THE COMPLETE FOOTBALL PASSING GAME

DON READ

Parker Publishing Company, Inc.
West Nyack, N. Y.

LIBRARY OF CONGRESS
CATALOG CARD NUMBER: 73–92590

PRINTED IN THE UNITED STATES OF AMERICA
BC–13–160036–2

Dedication

My Coach, Jim Underhill
My Friend, Fred Brock
My Brothers, Len and Dick
My Parents, Mr. and Mrs. C. E. Read
and
My Wife, Lois

What This Book Offers the Coach

The current trend toward throwing the ball in college and the influence of professional football increases the need for new ideas and strategies for the passing game. Prepared as a reference book on all phases of passing for any football program, this work features the "how-to" of basic fundamentals, advanced techniques, new ideas, proven strategy, workable drills, organizational materials, detailed play execution, and a practical football psychology for developing a pass attack.

This book also includes a complete, championship-tested program on quarterback, receivers, and linemen. More specifically, in strategy, it outlines and then details the various segments of a passing attack including the drop-back, sprint-out, and play-action passing forms.

Included in most of the chapters are various charts and diagrams that clarify the various points. One chapter is full of diagrams of drills that complement the passing game and insure exact timing and execution. Other chapters set forth daily work sheets, example practice schedules, forms used in practice and game organization, numerous pass routes, and specific plays.

In short, this book is intended as an A-to-Z guide to passing, including all the information and necessary nuts and bolts for the football coach to build his own high-scoring, ever-threatening passing offense.

——Don Read

Table of Contents

The Complete
Football Passing Game

1

Why a Successful
Passing Attack
Will Win Games for You

There is something fascinating about watching a football fly through the air while a receiver runs under it to gather it in! The perfected pass appeals to people today just as power football attracted crowds of yesteryear. The time when the biggest, strongest, team was always the victor is a thing of the past. In the passing game, speed and agility are as important, if not more so, than size. This is a time when football games are won by the team that makes the fewest mistakes; a period that stresses execution, sequence, strategy, psychology, and organization. Never before has scouting opponents been so important. Preparation for a specific game has become as crucial as the championship game of a few seasons ago. Such improvement has been made that football bears little resemblance to the game of thirty years ago. We are living in an age of science and technology—football has become a science! Those involved in coaching now employ an analytical and scientific approach.

Since the game has changed so radically over the years, it is only realistic to believe that it will advance even further in the years to come. If this be the case, coaches and those associated with football either will have to progress with it, or fall by the wayside. Of all phases of the game, it is the passing attack that has changed most. Football is moving very rapidly toward a wide-open variety of play. Thus the passing game must become the foundation of future competition. If you can accept this theory, adopting a passing philosophy will not be difficult. Those teams which adhere to and develop it will be leaders in the continuing development of the game of football.

REASONS FOR A PASSING GAME

The passing game provides a wide-open style of football. People enjoy watching a team that throws the ball. It is a brand of ball that spectators will return to see again and again. Fans do not tire of the explosive type football exhibited by a passing attack. Win or lose, the crowd always seems to leave the stadium content in that their time has been well spent.

If you analyze why people seem pleased with a team that passes, you will determine that people attend football games to be entertained. When they see a good pass offense in action, they have viewed football at its best. Fans are spoiled, since they can turn on television any weekend and see great professional football. Why should they go out and watch high school or college football that is not appealing? Who wants to see the offense that functions on the "three yards and a cloud of dust" philosophy? If we want fans, we must supply them with football that is colorful!

A more important reason for passing, from the coach's viewpoint, is that it will win games. Anyone who reads the sporting green can readily note that successful college and pro teams put the ball in the air. Teams like U.S.C., Notre Dame, U.C.L.A., and Michigan State throw the football, and year in and year out they are winners. There is no question about football becoming an aerial game.

Passing compensates for lack of speed and size

Presenting spectators with the brand of football they like is not the only reason for stressing the passing game in an offense. A few years ago our staff evaluated our player personnel for the coming season and decided that with a lack of size and speed we would have to throw the ball. (Please note that I use the words "would have to throw," because our feeling was that we did not have a choice.)

In accepting the hypothesis that there is need for either size or speed, and preferably both in a running offense, we decided that it would not be sound logic to maintain the philosophy of a strong running game without adequate material. Thus our staff, though believers in the running game, changed its concept of football. This change allowed us to win three consecutive league championships. We accepted the idea that passers and receivers can be made, with the proper teaching of players who are willing to spend a great deal of time working and practicing. We considered passing and receiving as skills—and skills can be mastered, perfected, and improved. Although this is contrary to what many coaches believe, this is the theory one must hold if the passing game is to be effective. This philosophy is not only necessary with the coaching staff of a team, but also it must be instilled in your players.

Players and coaches alike must realize that the most important element needed in any passing game is confidence. This feeling must be conveyed by the coaches. They have to believe in what they are trying to do. The coach must be a zealous person who is truly sold on this phase of the game. A coach cannot be passive about throwing the ball and expect a team to be enthusiastic.

PROMOTE THAT PASSING ATTACK!

If a coaching staff believes in the pass, selling players on the merits of this style of play is not difficult. Here are three methods that can be used:

(1) Compile statistics on other outstanding passing teams. These results can help prove the point that games can be won by throwing the ball. The average player will accept a philosophy more readily if the theories have been successful somewhere else. Since many of our nation's leading

college and high school teams have fine passing records, this feat is easily verified.

(2) Bring in a name quarterback from a college or professional team to discuss the values and merits of throwing the ball. This will sometimes impress the fellows more than will the words of the coach. Most teams are more than happy to send their quarterback for this purpose.

(3) Splice together old films of outstanding passing plays, making a film that evinces the great potential of the forward pass. This movie might include highlights of games of a team known for its passing, or perhaps film cuts of several teams that have utilized the forward pass.

Organizing a practice to emphasize the passing game can help make this phase of the program important. If, for example, the passing game is worked on daily rather than twice a week, it will surely make a meaningful impression upon the team. Also, if practices are set up to feature the passing game early in each daily routine, the importance of the forward pass is again pointed out. To the squad, placement of passing game practice and time alloted therefor will indicate, as well or better than any other method, where the emphasis of the offense lies.

It does not take long for a team to appreciate the threat presented by the forward pass. Once scores have been obtained with the bomb, the realization that the forward pass is a tremendous weapon becomes evident. A team can be behind one play, and with the next play it can move ahead. Passing can keep an inferior team in a game with a team far superior. A passing team does not have to maintain ball control, since every play is a potential first down or score.

MORE PASSING YET TO COME

The passing game in most sections of the country has not yet been intensely explored or utilized. In how many Saturday games, that you watch on television or attend in person, do you see the college or high school teams run the ball on first down, run the ball on second down, and then only if there is third down and long yardage, do you see the team go to the air? The fallacy in passing only on long yardage situations is that the opponent also knows it is a throwing situation. The result often is an ineffective pass attack. Why not throw on first down occasionally and then, if desired, run on second and third down? This plan would surely lead to a more effective attack, with the opposition uncertain as to when you are going to pass.

Another phase of the passing game that deserves emphasis is the psychological effect which the pass presents. The lift a team gets from a quick score through the air can allow a club the psychological edge often needed to win the game. A team that has the threat of the pass definitely possesses an advantage over the team that does not. In today's scientific game of football, scouts soon learn of a team's abilities, strengths, and weaknesses. Tendencies become apparent and they result in the opposition defending accordingly. There are teams today against which a nine-man front easily could be used because they do not have an effective passing game! This writer is not trying to be derogatory, but rather wishes to emphasize the need and importance of a sound passing game.

A passing offense lends itself to an efficient running offense. When a football team utilizes the forward pass, the running attack cannot help but be favorably affected. As a team becomes conscious of another team's passing offense, it must spend time preparing for the opponent's ability to throw. Thus, less time can be used in preparation for the running game. The end result should be that the running game will complement the throwing attack and become an effective part of the total offense.

WHAT IS NEEDED?

To make the running game go, a team needs size and/or speed. To make a successful passing game, you need only position on the defense. This physical position refers to: (1) the right position to throw from; (2) the proper position of receiver on defender; and (3) the correct position by blockers on defensive rushers. For these things, you do not need speed or size. A passing game, then, can be developed and perfected far beyond what the average coach might anticipate. Putting the ball in the air with accuracy and winning games can take place even with second rate talent. On the other hand, few teams that rely predominately on the running game win with inferior ability.

From field position, we can move directly on to the requirements for individual player placement complementary to the passing game. This placement might be splitting one end; it might mean splitting one end and flanking a back. And then again, a passing offense often flanks two backs or splits two ends. Adding a man-in-motion to any of the above sets is also common in a passing offense. Placing two backs and an end to the same side of the offense is becoming popular.

DEFENSIVE REACTION

The spreading of receivers tends to create a multitude of problems for the defense. Using split ends, flankers, and men-in-motion often forces opponents into un-normal or foreign pass coverage situations. For example, it might force a linebacker to cover a halfback, or a cornerbacker to cover a flanker. Generally, when a defensive player is placed in a position foreign to him, he will not be as effective as he would in a position he normally plays. Thus when an unusual adjustment is placed before a defensive secondary, the offense has an advantage. Using flankers and split ends might also force the poorest of a defensive secondary to cover the best offensive receiver. With motion, a secondary can be rotated out of position at times, or forced to change coverage at the last possible moment. Use of motion might also allow a given zone or area of the field to be flooded.

Double-wing formations, slot sets, and triple-wing sets will pose problems for a normal three-deep secondary. A four-deep secondary can have problems with a flanker set combined with a man-in-motion to the side the flanker sets. This, of course, provides a flood action to one side and again places the defensive secondary in an unusual placement. Motion also allows an offense the privilege of putting its best man against one of the weaker defensive backs.

Another consideration that deserves some thought is that spread type sets tend to take away the big rush or pressure on the passer. This is evident when defensive teams attempt to place a one-and-a-half or two-man coverage upon given receivers. By this it is meant that a corner blocker or end might drop off to help cover a good receiver. The result is less pressure on the running game or passer. For example, when a team covers another team's receivers with more than one man, it allows ten offensive men to play against nine defensive players, since a flanker or split end is used. This will limit the defense's containing ability and the offense will move the ball.

Forcing a team to drop off or place more than one man on a receiver gives the offense the advantage of running to the side of the defensive adjustment. This is generally very effective. Sweeping and running a power play at a cornerbacker removed or an end dropped off allows the offense a real edge since the defense no longer has the containment it had in a normal alignment. By using the wide set incorporating split ends and flankers the defense is prone to spread itself over a wider area. Defending this larger area is much more difficult than containing a standard "T" formation set. The enemy is forced to use either a five- or six-man front if it is to cover and defend the various zones and receivers. The aim is to put the opposition in a position where it cannot defend against the pass without weakening itself against the run.

THE FUTURE IS BRIGHT

There don't seem to be any limitations to the refinement of the forward pass. Its scope is far-reaching, and individual phases of the passing game are just currently being perfected and developed. New dimensions are emerging—the future of the forward pass looks bright! It is becoming the basis of offensive football; it is adding explosiveness to the game. This is what the American public wants and, since their demands usually dictate, it is reasonable to expect even greater emphasis on this phase of football.

A SUCCESSFUL PASSING ATTACK WILL WIN
GAMES FOR YOU!

2

Coaching the Passer

Most men who teach football today acquired their knowledge in an era when the forward pass was just something to turn to if the running game failed. Since most men coaching today did not play football when the passing game excelled, their background is limited and thus their coaching of this phase of football is restricted. And because the passing game was only a supplementary thing a few years ago, many coaches today have not yet accepted it. Being comparatively new to football, the aerial game is continually changing and improving. With new innovations comes an evolution in coaching techniques. Emphasis on some aspects of football increases while other phases of the game seem to be neglected. We feel very strongly that the fundamental skill of throwing the ball is one of these unemphasized areas. Practice sessions tend to concentrate on minute details and elaborate drills such as ways to stop a clock, goal line scoring, the kicking game, defending areas of the field, play sequence, wet weather procedures, game psychology, strategy and many others. While we admit all of these concerns need attention, they still distract from work on fundamental skills and a coach must establish a criteria for allotment of time when he favors a passing offense.

Provided adequate practice time is given a player, the skill of passing will be *easy* for him to master. Again it should be emphasized that with the proper physical tools, throwing the football is a simple task. The accepted theory, that "most kids can't pass," is one we avidly disagree with. In fact, we believe *most* can pass, and the task of passing is the easiest phase of the entire aerial game. Compared to play selection, faking, leadership, poise, and running ability, throwing the football is basic and elementary. More mistakes are made as a result of one of the previously mentioned elements than from the poorly thrown pass.

An inaccurate pass often stems from defensive pressure on the passer, poor execution of play-action, patterns being run incorrectly, improper faking or inclement weather. This statement may be hard to accept, for most of us tend to fix the blame for an ineffective passing attack on the passer. If, however, the entire pass offense is evaluated, more times than not the passer is not at fault when the throwing game bogs down.

The philosophy that we are trying to point out with respect to the art of passing is that throwers can become passers—that with enough practice *several* players on a squad may become good passers. The art of passing is only a skill. As stated in the previous chapter on philosophy of the passing game, skills can be developed, thus passers can and are made rather than born.

It is conceded that, during the fall of the year, coaches rarely have time to work on a drill allowing some of the unknowns to throw. It is during the spring or summer that this feat might be accomplished. We believe that potential passers are on every campus of the country. If coaches are willing to look, discover, and work with these prospects, passers can be developed. Once a passer has been discovered, there remains continuous work and development until his full potential is realized.

The worth of a passer should not be based solely upon the number of passes completed, but rather upon the number of interceptions thrown. Our observations over the years have shown us that the good passer does not always throw the "beautiful" pass or have the strong arm. The real measure of a passer is his ability to get the ball to the receiver with enough lead and at the correct time. To accomplish this, a passer must possess certain qualifications, three of which are discussed at length in the following paragraphs.

BASIC REQUIREMENTS FOR A PASSER

First, he must have *quick hands*. This is imperative since quick hands allow the ball to be delivered at the correct time. So many of today's passers get the ball to the receiver either late or early. There is nothing quite as discouraging as to see a receiver wide open, but then covered by the time the ball arrives; or to have the football on its way to the receiver who has not looked toward the passer and seen the ball. Poor hands can cause improper timing of the throw and lead to interceptions and incomplete passes.

Another qualification for a good passer is *peripheral vision*. A passer has a tremendous advantage if he can see the entire field of play. Knowing where both the primary and secondary receivers are is not enough. The great passer will not only *know* where the receivers are but will also be able to *see* them. This enables the passer to pick out and throw to the appropriate receiver, preventing interceptions and increasing the number of completions. It is unlikely that a passer with peripheral vision will throw to a receiver who is covered, and very probably he will hit the receiver who is open.

The third requirement for a good passer is *agility*. It is one thing to stand back and throw the ball from a set position and still another to pass under pressure, perhaps off balance and moving to avoid the defensive rush. To accomplish this a passer must be well coordinated, with the ability to recover when knocked around. Like the two previously mentioned requirements, agility is difficult to develop and tends to be more a natural thing.

When a passer has good hands, peripheral vision and agility, he is going to be great. He will not have his passes intercepted often and he will complete a high percentage of his passes. There are, however, some other contributing factors to good passing.

ADDITIONAL FUNDAMENTAL REQUIREMENTS

Closely linked with good hands, peripheral vision and agility is *proper control* of the football while readying to pass. To insure good control of the ball, it is necessary that both hands have a secure grip on the ball. Yes, a passer can hold the ball with one hand, but it is difficult and dangerous. A pass that is not thrown "true" because of the wobble of the ball, more than likely resulted from a wrist that did not remain straight. A pass that falls short is generally caused by the nose of the ball going down. These and many other difficulties in passing come from trying to throw the ball without the use of the guide hand.

Position of the hand on the ball

There are many acceptable methods of holding a football. Some of the great passers of this era have very unorthodox ways of gripping a ball. The size of hands, type of football, kind of exchange from center, and weather conditions, all affect a passer's hand position on the football. A passer with small hands may tend to hold the ball closer to the back point, while the large-handed thrower generally will grip the football closer to the middle of the ball.

The make and size of football is directly related to how the ball is held. Even though most colleges today use the same ball, there are many high schools and some colleges that are not restricted to a specific one. Rubber and leather footballs have different feels. Seams differ in height, as does the specific shape of footballs. There are at least two footballs on the market today that are one-quarter inch smaller in diameter than two widely known makes. These factors surely contribute to where the hand is placed on the ball.

There are, however, some guidelines that can be used to determine the position of the passing hand on the ball. The hand should be placed in a position on the ball that feels most comfortable to the passer. The middle of the hand, though, should never extend to the forward part of football. Rather, it should be placed normally slightly to rear of middle of the ball.

It is absolutely imperative that the football not rest in the palm of the hand. The ball must be held with the fingers, thumb and heel of hand. If this rule is not followed the passer will have limited touch or feel of the ball. When a wobbly pass occurs, improper hand position may be the reason.

Spacing the fingers at the correct interval is another must for effective hand position. Length of fingers of course has a lot to do with finger spacing. Generally though the wider the spreading of the fingers, the better the control of the ball. Since controlling the ball is only part of the skill of passing, a thrower should not overextend his fingers to the point where they are not comfortable. Rather he should experiment until a good feeling position is determined.

Keeping the wrist straight

We believe the most fundamental necessity in throwing the ball is keeping the wrist straight. This can be proven if one will relate it to how a pitcher makes a baseball curve—by turning the wrist the ball is forced to spin, and as the spinning ball turns in the air it meets resistance which causes it to break. When throwing a football, there must not be a twist of the wrist. To insure this, a passer needs to use the other hand to keep the ball and throwing hand in position. The end result will be a good, true pass.

Using the second hand on the ball also insures that the ball will be kept at the proper height and correct distance from the body. A common fault of passers is to let the ball get too close to the body, thus losing the freedom of the throwing arm. When the ball is allowed to be dropped lower than the throwing position, a poor pass will result. Again, it should be stressed that the second hand on the ball can eliminate many of these passing problems.

We like to teach our passer to push the ball away from his ear with the left hand (if right handed) until he feels the ball is ready to be thrown. The longer the pass, the harder the push. When the push on the ball is hard, the nose of the ball will be forced up. This of course is desirable on a longer pass. The guide hand's pressure on the ball should come from the heel of the hand and be directed upward and outward through the ball.

Faking

The second hand can also be used to aid in faking with the ball, while retaining good position. By batting the ball against the second hand, a good fake can be made and the grip on the ball can be retained. It is suggested though that faking with the ball be done not more than twice on a long pass and only once on a short throw. When using this technique we instruct our passer to make the initial fake in a direction other than that in which the ball will be thrown. If this feint is carried out, it will tend to hold the defensive secondary and sometimes help influence defensive flow in a direction away from the primary pattern.

Balance

Another fundamental needed by a passer is good balance which can determine whether a throw will be accurate or not. The weight of the body must be placed on the back leg (right leg right handed, left leg left handed). It is important that there be a slight bend at the knee since this allows the passer's body to establish the weight on the back leg. This position also aids in the transferring of weight to the front leg as the arm comes forward to throw. The balance phase of passing is completed after the passer steps in the direction of the receiver and releases the ball as his weight is shifted to the front foot. (The follow-through phase of passing is discussed in some detail later in this chapter.)

Extending the front arm away from the body as the ball is being released is another technique that helps maintain good balance. The height of arm is determined by the depth of the pass. The longer the pass, the higher the arm should point. The arm can be bent at the elbow or extended completely, whichever feels most comfortable to the passer.

The extension of the front arm should begin as the passing arm starts backward. It is important that both hands remain on the ball until the passer moves his passing arm away from his chest to coil for the throw. Failure to keep the ball covered with both hands in the setting-up stage of passing can encourage fumbles.

Maintaining correct balance is imperative not only to throw the ball well, but to allow the best possible position for the passer to absorb the blows of onrushing linemen. Proper balance when passing can prevent injuries as well as allow pass completions.

Arc of arm

Let us first state that we do not feel there is a specific path the arm should follow when throwing the football. Each and every passer acquires a motion most natural for himself. Our opinion is that when working with passers, overcoaching is the most dangerous thing that can happen. The vital concern when teaching passers is that the ball be thrown true, with enough height and velocity. If these aspects of passing are not present, it is then necessary to do some coaching. We think that coaching a passer primarily deals with correcting problems or poor habits. Typical errors in fundamental arm action are: 1) Not getting the arm away from the body; 2) Not bringing the arm all the way through the arc; and 3) Improper position of the ball while in the arc.

Again we want to state that some of the better passers of our time have been semi-sidearmers. Trying to change a passer's style is difficult, and sometimes more problems are created than gains made. When working with a passer, the proper function of the coach is to advance the boy's individual style, not to impose someone else's upon him.

Follow-through

A common error, regularly made when passing, is not bringing the arm and fingers through in their natural follow-through motion. Accuracy of passing is dependent upon this portion of the skill of throwing. Follow-through action of the arm includes bringing the arm over the shoulder and then locking the elbow as the ball leaves the hand of the passer. When the arm is not locked at the elbow, the full range of the arm has not been used—and a snap pass, which is rarely on target, results. Passers who try to deliberately throw the soft pass sometimes fail to lock the elbow and a snap throw occurs.

A second consideration regarding follow-through is the position and location of fingers as the ball leaves the hand of the passer. If the fingers of the passing hand are not pointed in the direction of the receiver as ball starts on its course, the passer has not followed through. Here again the result may be an unsuccessful pass. We find that a good way to determine a passer's finger follow-through is to take either still photos or motion pictures of his arm and hand action. The passer can witness his own difficulties and learn a great deal.

Following through when passing involves more than the arm and hand action. As the arm begins its cycle action, the weight of the body must also compliment the movement of the arm. The weight of the body, which is placed on the rear leg, must be shifted to the front leg as the arm completes its revolvement in the throwing process. The transferring of weight from one leg to the other is very similar to a batter in baseball swinging at a ball—like the hitter, the passer starts with his weight on the rear leg. By pushing off the back leg, the distribution of weight is sent up the rear leg to the hips and other leg. As the push-off begins, the front leg will be lifted to aid the process of transferring weight. During the transferment of weight, the back leg will be bent slightly at the knee. This is important since the bend in the back leg serves as a coil from which to spring. The front leg is kept straight, with the toe of the foot pointing to the intended direction of the pass.

While in the set position, readying to start the arm into action, weight should rest almost solely on the ball of the back foot. As this weight is transferred, it should be shifted to the ball of the front foot. It is important that little or no weight be placed on the heel since weight distributed to the heels puts the thrower in an unbalanced position.

As the weight shifts to the front leg, hips must whip the upper torso to allow the arm to follow through. This action puts power into the pass by helping the body follow the arm through its course. The degree of hip action is determined by the direction of the step of the front foot. The more "open" the step, the more hip action received. If the step is not open or in the same direction, the passing arm is "traveling," hip action is restrained and follow-through is not possible. (Another way of saying this is that the passer is throwing against his body.)

CONCLUSION

We maintain that passing, like any other skill, will improve with practice. Of the literature written concerning the pros and cons of passing, the classical statement that appears so often is: "Throwers are a dime a dozen—passers are one in a thousand." We do not accept this theory. Rather, we believe that the success of a passer depends upon his physical ability and the stress placed on the art itself by those coaching him. Throwing the football is an elementary process, but because many passers are not given the opportunity to throw often enough or with proper instruction, they never cultivate their potential. There is a direct correlation between time spent on a given phase of the game and success in that aspect of football. Therefore, a passer's record will reflect what he has done on the practice field. The team's aerial success depends, without question, on its passers.

3

Coaching the Receiver

Get open—catch the football—run! This, in essence, is what pass receiving is all about. But contrary to what many people think, this is not simple. Good pass catchers are more difficult to come by than good passers. Only a small percentage of those who come out for football have the attributes to become capable receivers. A receiver must possess two general ingredients if he is to be effective: He needs, first, the physical qualifications; and second, the rare mental and emotional stability few young men possess.

Physical necessities should include agility, speed, size, and of course, good hands. Often we get a boy who has some of these qualities, but lacks others. The number of passes he will catch will certainly relate directly to his physical qualifications. Some of the above physical elements, however, can be improved upon with work and proper coaching. It is only realistic, though, to admit that physical attributes can be developed only to the potential of a footballer's natural physical qualities.

The second aspect of pass receiving has to do with a receiver's mental and emotional state. It is our opinion that this phase of pass receiving can be perfected and improved upon tremendously. A definition of mental and emotional stability as it applies to pass receiving, is—the frame of mind or outlook a receiver has about catching the football. The mental phase of pass receiving involves the personality of a boy—including confidence, poise, intelligence, and intestinal fortitude.

Mental qualities of a receiver, however, cannot be measured in a passing drill. Rather, they are either discovered or found lacking under game conditions. Add a defensive secondary, and the task of receiving becomes *most* difficult. The reason pass receiving is so difficult is pass defense.

Pass defenders contain pass receiving in a number of ways. Restrictions placed on a receiver often start at the line of scrimmage. It is here that many passing plays are broken up, when receivers are prevented from releasing or running their desired course—and harassed, in many cases, throughout their entire route—molested *up to* and *as* they are taking possession of the ball. These are the most notable obstacles that challenge pass receivers.

FUNDAMENTALS OF PASS RECEIVING

There are five fundamental phases to pass receiving. Each of these phases must be considered important and worked on independently if the pass receiver is to run a successful route and catch the ball. These fundamentals need daily drill.

Releases

With the great emphasis today on holding up receivers, it is becoming more difficult for a receiver to get by the defender. To accomplish this feat the receiver must be well schooled in basic maneuvers that will allow him to get by the defensive man. Some of the better techniques to aid release are:

1) Scramble—stay on all fours and scramble by the defensive man.

2) Head fake—step in one direction and release in the other direction while motioning with the head.

3) Fake block—throw a shoulder into the man, but release immediately.

4) Spin—keeping the knees high and legs wide apart, the receiver releases in a spin and rolls off the defensive man.

    5) Limp leg—step at the defensive man and then pull the lead leg away as the receiver steps into the defensive man with the other leg.

Fakes

There are many effective forms of faking. Obviously, the type of fake a receiver might use should depend upon the pattern being run, the way the defensive man is playing the receiver, and the specific moves of the receiver. There are, however, some rudimental moves that can be used by almost any receiver.

    1) Head fake—the receiver jerks his head in one direction and then cuts in another direction.

THIS TYPE ✱   2) Hand fake—using the hands to emphasize a direction and
FAKE SHOULD   then turning and sprinting in another direction. Usually the
NOT BE USED   hands are brought over the head or at least shoulder high.
WHEN SPEED
ESSENTIAL   3) Change-of-pace fake—the receiver runs at half or three-
ON A DEEP   quarter speed and then, when near the defender, sprints past him.

    4) Cut fake—the receiver runs in one direction, plants a foot and cuts in another direction—foot away from the direction of the pattern should be planted.

    5) Multi-cut procedure—the receiver makes two or more plants and cuts in different directions. Generally a multiple cut pattern will have to be a shorter route because of the time it consumes.

    6) Stop technique—the receiver runs a course straight downfield and, at a predetermined point, plants his outside foot and turns to face the passer. The move can be a sign move or it might be the first phase of a pattern. For example, the hook pass, hook-go pass, hook-slide-in pass, and hook-slide-out pass are each started by the stop technique. This maneuver is an easy one and yet it causes the defense a lot of problems.

    7.) STOP & GO or HITCH & GO

Running the pattern

A third aspect of pass receiving is the running phase. After the initial fake has been made, the receiver must maintain the good position he has acquired on the defender and try to outrun him. If the play is timed well, the ball should be released shortly after the fake has been made (within the first five steps of the receiver's route on most patterns).

Catching the ball

The most basic element of pass catching is first getting one's body in line with the flight of the ball. To accomplish this, the receiver must keep his eye on the front point of the ball until it reaches his hands. The final phase of catching is getting the hands up and bringing in the ball. Hands must be extended away from the body in a receiving position. We refer to this as *looking the ball into hands.* As important as receiving the ball is allowing some "give" with the fingers when the ball strikes the hands, to make the soft catch. After the catch is made, the last action is covering up the ball with the arms and hands.

Hand positioning is most important. After the ball has left the passer's hands and is enroute, a receiver needs to hold his hands in a position that will best allow receiving the pigskin. Sometimes it might mean one hand being fixed higher than the other, or getting both hands up or down, depending on the height of the ball. A general rule on any ball caught above the waist is that the thumbs should be to the inside; on balls caught below the hips, the thumbs should be facing outside. Regardless of the position of the thumbs, it is most important to keep the fingers apart or outstretched. This position helps hands act as a net to capture the ball.

Running with the ball

Being a ballcarrier after a catch is made is almost as important as the skills described previously. Often a defense has only one or two defenders to stop the offense after a catch is made. Whenever the ballcarrier has but one or two of his opposition to contend with, his chances of getting big yardage or even a score are good.

RECEIVER TECHNIQUES

Closely related to fundamental or basic phases of pass receiving is the use of various techniques and maneuvers. All receivers have specific maneuvers they perform well. Mastering these techniques will classify receivers into the categories of good or fair. A good receiver excels in executing these maneuvers and frequently finds himself in the open.

Maneuvers used by pass receivers to open up a pattern or isolate a defender are important if a receiver is to catch many passes. It is one thing to draw a good-looking pass pattern on the blackboard or have a receiver run drills practicing the route, and quite another to successfully execute the play under game conditions. The point is that maneuvers taught a receiver should be as close to game conditions as possible. For example, a pass catcher should work frequently against live defenders even if the drill is completely dummy. Again the objective is to make the situation realistic.

Techniques developed by receivers while in the route of a pattern are varied and numerous. There are, however, basic moves that are applicable to any or all receivers. These methods can be used against any form of defensive coverage. They are also successful against a defensive back with great speed and agility as well as an average defensive back. Some of these elementary but important techniques are listed as follows:

> *Change of speed*   This technique is a maneuver involving a receiver running down field at three-four speed, then quickening his pace in an attempt to outrun the defensive man. The change of speed is mainly used on streak patterns.

> *Use of head*   Use of the head in "taking" a defender is a most commonly used method. The receiver simply throws his head in one direction while planting one foot and driving in another direction.

> *Use of hands*   Like the head fake, hands help free a defensive man and allow the receiver to get that extra step on the

secondary. This fake starts when the receiver throws his hands up or places his hands in a receiving position, then sprints away from defenders.

Slide   After a hook pattern has been run, a receiver can slide in one direction or another. The slide move is difficult to cover and is a hard maneuver to make. The slide involves starting away from the hook after it has been made.

Use of eyes   Looking away from direction of initial cut is a commonly used technique. This method is particularly effective on a deep pattern involving a single break. An example would be a deep-out pattern. On this course the receiver can look in one direction and cut in another.

Fake block move   This skill involves a receiver starting toward a defensive man as if to block him and, at the last possible second, breaking into a pattern. Normally this move is used off the play action pass and is a short-type pattern.

Plant foot and drive   Of all maneuvers presented, planting the foot is perhaps the most often relied on technique. The maneuver begins with the receiver running a pattern right at a defensive man and when as close to him as possible, planting a foot and driving off in a given direction. If the drive is to outside the receiver plants inside foot. If the drive is to inside, outside foot is planted.

Complementary pattern look   This is running a pattern in a lazy manner so as to give the defender the idea the ball will be thrown to someone else. Usually a receiver runs this course at about one-half speed until ready to make his cut to receive ball.

Multiple cut technique   Consisting of more than one cut or break, this is very difficult to defend against. Of all pass patterns, this form of pass generally takes the most time. Multiple cut techniques are used in zorro patterns, sideline-and-up, hook-and-go.

Drag leg technique   Used as a change of pace technique, a receiver runs right at defensive man and when near him, drags one leg for a step. This tends to freeze the defensive man as he anticipates a cut. It is a good way to get by a defender on a streak pattern.

Drop shoulder method   Used primarily with the plant foot technique, as a receiver approaches defensive secondary man he simply drops one shoulder to give impression of moving one way, then breaks in another direction.

Screen technique   This is used only on limited patterns. It is most effective off a cutting pattern. A sideline or out pattern run at twelve yards will screen a defender from a receiver that runs a pattern at five or six yards. Another form of screen can come off a square-in pattern by having another receiver run a hook pattern underneath the cutting pattern.

There are specific fundamentals that a receiver can adhere to in order to improve and develop the aforementioned aptitudes in his receiving. These basic rules apply to both the little back and the big end. Some of these fundamentals are often violated by great receivers, but nevertheless are necessary and pertinent to any good passing team. Every receiver should follow these basics at least until he has perfected his abilities.

PASS RECEIVING RULES

1) Keep hands relaxed.
2) Keep eye on ball once it leaves hands of passer.
3) Catch ball with hands without aid of body.
4) Get best possible position on ball.
5) Look ball into hands.
6) Thumbs in on high catches and out on low catches.

When incorporating the rules, a receiver should try, whenever possible, to get the defender to cross his feet. Once this has happened the receiver can make his break and place the defender at a great disadvantage. This theory is basic but not necessary. The most important thing a receiver can do to get open is to run his regular route, making his break according to yards needed and the abilities of the defender. The better receivers in the game seldom make multiple fakes to get open. Today, the passing game is becoming more a matter

of timing; that is, being in the right place at the right time
and having the ball thrown at the correct time.

Receiver mistakes

Of the mistakes a receiver can make, taking his eye off the
ball is the most severe. A common occurrence is that of a receiver glancing away to determine the location of his defenders, thus losing the ball. This quick look often surrenders
a possible offensive gain. Therefore, it is imperative to instill
in your receivers the philosophy of *first*, catching the ball and
second, running with it. In order to do this a receiver must
have some natural instinct. It takes instinct to know where the
defensive secondary is without removing the eyes from the flight
of the ball. But a player's best assets here are confidence in his
ability and a little intestinal fortitude!

Taking one's eyes off the ball is occasionally caused by an
improper route to the ball. If the pattern is not run correctly, the receiver may be in a poor position to see the football. Therefore, maintaining proper alignment with the ball
can be directly related to the way a course is run. If the pattern
is run right, a receiver's main objective after his last break is to
get a bearing on the passer and the ball. As the pigskin
leaves the hand of the thrower, it should be brought into focus.
This aspect is the most crucial part of this entire phase of receiving. From observation, it is our belief that more passes are
dropped due to a receiver taking his eye off the ball than for any
other reason.

A second error receivers routinely make is looking toward
the line of scrimmage or passer too early in the pattern. This
mistake not only slows up the receiver, but it serves to key the
defensive people as to the point of reception. Obviously,
this rule does not apply when a quick pass is being thrown.

CONCLUSION

To catch the pigskin, one must have the desire to do so, and
then be willing to work hard at developing the skill. Productive

pass grabbing will occur only after improper techniques are eliminated and sound fundamentals established. Daily repetition of the rudimental aspects of pass receiving is the only way to excellence. Once adequate receiving is apparent, other phases of the passing game can be considered. It should be remembered, however, that with completions come wins!

4

Developing Formations
for Passing Attacks

There is *no* passing game if proper passing formations are not adhered to. Trying to establish a throwing attack without using appropriate sets is like throwing from dropback action without pass protection. A team must first adopt certain offensive sets before any forms of offensive plays can be considered.

The question is, what criteria should be used to determine the best formations? Though coaches may disagree as to exactly which sets are more suitable, most teachers of the passing game tend to be in agreement on several specifics. A passing attack needs four primary ingredients. They are the passer, receivers, pass protection blockers, and appropriate sets. Formations selected should be based upon the first three elements. In the abilities of these individuals lies the potential, but *how the potential is used* determines success or failure. Position placement is strongly influenced by the qualifications of the players, as are the number and kind of sets.

It is of little value to split an end or flank a back ten yards and not throw the ball to him. An offense has gained an advantage over the defense by splitting a man, but this edge is reduced if the man is not used as a receiver. Likewise, using a man-in-motion or setting two backs as slots or wings is ridiculous if they are not used as receivers. There is little value in sprinting out with the quarterback if this footballer can't both pass and run. It is poor judgment to throw deep if the passer does not have a strong arm or the pass protection blockers are not capable of sustaining their blocks.

Thus, the number and kind of sets definitely should be related to the personnel available. This factor influences not only a formation, but the type of plays incorporated into the system. Assuming that appropriate talent is at hand, let us proceed into various positions within the sets and the formations themselves.

There are many types of sets that support a passing attack. Basically, however, a formation from which to pass must be one that provides for detached personnel. It must allow split ends, flanked backs, slotted, as well as wingbacks, in formations. An exact placement of detached personnel should be governed by their capabilities.

Some of the more widely used and successful passing formations are shown in Figures 4-1 to 4-4. These sets accomplish the aforementioned objectives of spreading people out, thus allowing for a wide-open passing game. Figures 4-1 and 4-2 are diagrams of one of the most commonly used formations in football, the Pro Set. The sets shown in Figures 4-3 and 4-4 represent formations that are being accepted more and more each year. There are, of course, other formations that are not

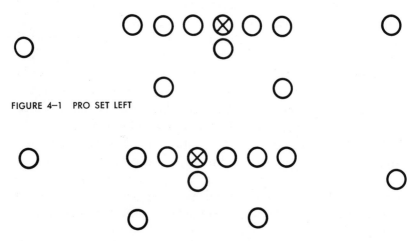

FIGURE 4–1   PRO SET LEFT

FIGURE 4–2   PRO SET RIGHT

The splits of wide receivers should vary depending on field position, specific play, weather conditions, and abilities of players involved.

discussed but relate well to the passing game, such as the double slot and triple wing made popular in recent years by some of the great passing teams in this country.

USE OF A FLANKER

A flankerback is the common name used for a back who lines up somewhere outside of his own offensive end and one yard behind the line of scrimmage. The distance of the split may vary from three to fifteen yards. Generally the exact location of a flanker is determined by field position. Obviously, flanking distance must be relative to the sideline. The closer a team sets to the sideline shrinks the distance at which a flanker sets.

Certain patterns will also dictate the distance a flanker splits. For instance, a square-out would not enable a flanker to take a large split, while a look-in pattern may require a wider split. On some running plays flankerbacks can be used as decoys by splitting extra wide and isolating one or two of the defensive secondary. Flankers can, on certain plays, be key blockers. This is particularly true on sweep action or reverse plays and, on occasion, downfield.

A footballer selected to play flanker must be versatile. This unique back should be the best receiver on a team, since the

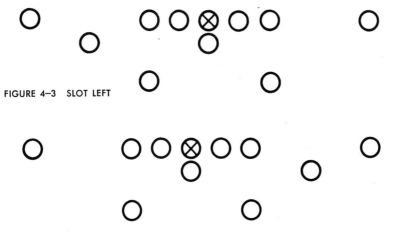

FIGURE 4–3   SLOT LEFT

FIGURE 4–4   SLOT RIGHT

Backfield alignment should vary with needs and philosophy. Most teams are using the "I" alignment, set backs, and strong formation.

ball generally will be thrown to him more than any other receiver. But being a good receiver is not enough. A flanker-back must be able to run with the ball once he gets it. Unlike an end, he is not often used to block, thus he does not have to be a giant. A flanker must have speed, agility, and aggressiveness. One who possesses these assets provides an offense with a real threat.

Why use flankers?

We feel that a passing offense must incorporate some form of flanker system. Keeping all backs in the backfield allows a defense to concentrate itself and defend a smaller area so that the passing game is restricted. By using a back as a flanker, many positive possibilities are present. (It should also be injected here that flanking one back normally does not detract from the running game. An offense can run or throw with equal effectiveness in either direction while using a flanker.) Using a flanker allows for combination pass patterns. Against zone coverage, combination routes are effective. Combination patterns are run with two or more receivers running different routes. One pattern usually clears a given area for the receiver who is to make the catch. A commonly used combination pattern is a cross-out or cross-in pattern. These cross-action patterns clear a zone by forcing the secondary to cover a decoy receiver running the streak pattern. Cutting behind the streak pattern is the receiver who will be in the clear if the secondary people are covering the deepest receiver in their zone.

There are, of course, many other forms of combination routes that are effective against zone coverage. Patterns involving hook-and-slide, down-and-back, Zorro, and V-out (which are shown in another chapter of this text) all can be complemented by another receiver running a pattern that clears the specific area where the pigskin will be thrown.

Use of a flanker often encourages defenses to cover flankers with more than one defender. Man-and-a-half or double coverage on flankers strengthens the running game, since the defense is then defending against it with fewer people. This form of coverage also tends to help a passing game since it often relieves coverage on other receivers and allows throwing to ends or remaining backs.

Flanking a man prevents the back from being held up at or behind the line of scrimmage. This quick release allows immediate or quick patterns to be run. One of the most difficult patterns to stop is a look-in. With a flanker there is always the potential of a quickly developing route to the inside.

A flanker can force the defense to rotate into an unsatisfactory defending position. Rotation can force the poorest of a defensive secondary to cover the best receiver, the slowest defender on the faster receiver. No rotation or an improper rotation can isolate one defensive man to cover one offensive man. This situation places the defense at a tremendous disadvantage, for when a defender is isolated, he has a much wider area to cover before getting help from a teammate.

Flankerbacks certainly add punch to an offense and place the defense in unadvantageous positions. More than any other factor, use of the flanker has changed the game of football and has helped make it wide open. A defense is compelled to spread its coverage to a flanker side, creating an inadequate defensive perimeter.

THE SPLIT END

Like a flanker, the split end spreads himself away from the main body offense in order to (1) force a beneficial rotation on defensive secondary; (2) allow sufficient room for the receiver to maneuver; or (3) encourage the defense to cover a split end with more than one defender. If any or all of these goals take place, use of the split end is an advantage.

Yardage involved in splits should be determined by a number of factors. Certainly the position on the field is of importance when determining such a split—if on the left hashmark the area to the left restricts the distance of split; on the other hand, if the offense is located on right hashmark, an area between the end and the tackle can be great.

The type of play called has influence on the position of an

end. If the end is expected to block on a given play, he must be stationed within range of his assignment. But if used as a decoy, the split end may take an abnormal split to influence defensive alignment. Splitting a little or a great deal may aid certain pass patterns by giving position to the receiver before the play begins.

Still another reason for splitting an end is to prevent a receiver from being blocked or held up at the line of scrimmage—the split end having more room to maneuver. Holding up receivers at the line of scrimmage is very common when an end is not spread. Being able to release immediately is clearly most important.

THE TIGHT END

Although many sound passing teams split both ends to put pressure on the pass defensive coverage, most successful passing teams like to keep one end in the normal end alignment. By spreading but one end, the running game is strengthened by using this player as a key blocker. It is also felt that a tight end can and should be an important receiver in any throwing attack. We have found that a tight end can be particularly effective on shorter pass patterns.

On routes such as hooks, look-ins, or square-ins, the big strong kid can often out-muscle a defender for the ball. A big tight end is likewise an easier target for the passer to hit. And lastly, this receiver is very effective in delayed patterns, since he is so often used as a blocker. Thus having size and strength in this footballer results in a better overall passing game.

USING SET-BACKS AS RECEIVERS

Regardless of the offensive set, an offensive must be able to utilize its set-backs as receivers. Set-backs are those backfieldmen stationed somewhere between offensive tackles and three or more yards deep. These backs should be used as both primary and secondary receivers. In other words, these backs must run predetermined routes and serve as receivers to whom the ball will be thrown. They must also act to catch a pass when it is not possible to throw to the prime receiver. Thus, remaining or set-backs are an important phase of any passing game.

Set-backs as blockers

Just as important as set-backs being good receivers is their blocking. There are very few passing plays where at least one of the remaining backs is not a blocker—there are many plays in which two backs must block. This is one reason that good passing teams select bigger, stronger set-backs.

The better blocker of the two set-backs should be positioned to the side of the removed end. Placing a stronger footballer here tends to counteract the quicker rush often received from the split end side. Various blocking techniques for these backs are discussed in Chapter 7.

A FORMATION MUST PROVIDE FOR MOTION

The man-in-motion can be the greatest asset an offense might have. If this statement be true, why then don't more teams capitalize on such an innovation? Theory and application seem simple enough, yet few teams incorporate the use of motion in their systems of play.

Our contention is that football has become so complex that it is necessary to establish rigid rules that help those who coach and play to determine responsibilities. These rules have particularly been exploited offensively. The adoption of fixed assignments for each player has limited the use of a man-in-motion and encouraged utilizing backs as blockers and decoys.

With the trend toward flanking a back to one side or another, backfield alignment has been restricted to two runners. Using but two running backs discourages having a man-in-motion, since it limits offensive flexibility.

Though both of the aforementioned factors may be in part true, we believe nevertheless that a man-in-motion adds punch rather than detracts from an offense. Involvement of motion not only creates variety, but it provides an offense with wide-open explosiveness and imagination not found in an offense of traditional nature. If, however, motion is to be effective, it must be utilized in all aspects of offense.

Motion man as blocker

A motion man can and should be used as a blocker. The back-in-motion can be an effective pass blocker or lead blocker in a running play. This endeavor can be accomplished by using a short form of motion. For example, the quarterback can put a back in motion and, when he is in the desired position, call an appropriate starting count to put play into action. From this place he can carry out the predetermined assignment.

Motion man as runner

It is as important to use the motion man as a runner as it is to have him block. There are two good ways the motion man can be used as a runner: First, to give him the ball while in motion and have him run an inside reverse or trap-type play; second, to pitch and hand off to him while he is in motion and have him carry the ball on a sweep play.

Motion man as receiver

Without a doubt the most profitable way to utilize a man-in-motion is to throw to him. By using both long and short motion this can easily be carried out. A variety of paths can be run from this in-motion position. The advantages of throwing to the motion man are at least threefold: (1) the secondary man may not properly rotate to cover this receiver; (2) the man-in-motion has a running start as play begins which enables him to get to a desirable position sooner; and (3) throwing to the motion man often places the defense in a disadvantageous position. Motion can force a defense to cover an offense's best man with the defense's poorest. This edge, in itself, is worth having a man-in-motion in an offense.

Motion man as decoy

A last way to involve the motion man is to use him as a decoy. If a team will rotate to the side where motion is directed, other pass patterns may open up. For example, if the motion from the left side of an offense causes a defensive rotation to its own left, a quick pass or throw-back pass to the left side becomes very effective. Long motion also can serve well as a decoy by causing a wide position placement of the defensive secondary.

NAMING THE BACKS

It has been our experience that if a specific name is given a back it will serve two purposes: (1) to identify a man in a given position; and (2) to enable a man-in-motion call to be simplified. Any short, easy-to-remember name will be sufficient. Names which have been satisfactory for us are:

RIGHT HALF——"Rip"
LEFT HALF——"Lou"
FULLBACK——"Fred"

When we want to place one of these backs in motion, we simply call the play and then state the back's name we wish to be in motion. A typical play might be 28 Power-*Rip*. This puts Rip in motion to the call side. If we want Rip in motion away from the call side, the call is 28 Power-*Rip Away*.

The distance the man-in-motion will run depends upon how he is to be used. If the man-in-motion is a decoy, maybe a longer motion is desired. If this be true, a quarterback delays the starting count until the motion man is in the correct position.

UTILIZING YOUR PERSONNEL

If a team is to incorporate any phase of the passing formation philosophy previously mentioned, appropriate personnel *must* be used in their best-suited positions. When a team sets in a Pro Formation-Right, the tight end positions himself in the right end position, while the split end lines up to the left. When a Pro Set is to the left, both ends then flop over and assume the other's position. This allows for needed specialization in a modern passing attack.

Besides changing the ends' positions on various sets, it is imperative that the remaining backs be placed correctly. As suggested earlier, this means keeping the bigger, stronger back positioned to the split end side, regardless of formation.

A flankerback's talents can best be used by flopping him from one side to the other. This procedure will place the key person in the vital position. Through flip-flopping personnel, better utilization will occur, and a more effective offense will result. A high degree of specialization leads to perfection. Perfection determines success . . . it's the formation that counts!

5

Coaching Techniques
of Drop-Back Passing

Regardless of the type of offense a football team employs, using some form of the drop-back pass is extremely important. The drop-back action pass not only supplies a team with shorter combination patterns, quick single routes, check-off passes, draw plays, and Statue of Liberty plays, but sets up key running plays.

The draw play and screen pass are two of the most explosive plays in football. It takes the drop-back action to set up these types of plays. Therefore, a team that depends strictly upon the sprint-out or play-action pass rarely utilizes the draw or screen. This does not mean the draw or screen cannot be used from these other forms of passing action; but it is questionable how effective a team will be without the drop-back action.

WHY PASS FROM DROP-BACK ACTION?

Selling the merits of this form of passing is easy, because it has stood the test of years at all levels of football. Professionals have perfected the drop-back pass to a highly developed stage which today constitutes the core of their offense. Many colleges and high schools alike have adopted this "trademark" from the pros.

There are two major categories of grouping drop-back passing plays: those plays designed to produce a score and those to get short yardage. A drop-back pass offense needs both these types of plays. Often the shorter route complements the scoring pattern since it may tend to hold a defender. The longer pass pattern might clear a zone or area for the shorter patterns to be run. Shorter passes include hook, sideline, look-in, flare, down-and-back, square-in, V-out, slide, and screen. Some longer passes needed in a drop-back pass offense are hook-go, out-and-up, Zorro, streak, square-out-deep, square-in-deep, and other multiple cut patterns. All of these patterns are diagramed in a later section of the book.

As important as patterns in a drop-back pass offense is the action of play itself. One real advantage of using the drop-back pass is that a passer is in a much better position to see the entire field of play. When passing from either the sprint-out or play-action styles, a passer's vision is limited to one side of the field, the side toward which his body is turned. The drop-back technique allows the passer to have his body pointed directly upfield.

Still another positive feature of the drop-back method is that most passers can throw more accurately from a set position. Proper weight distribution and balance can be established and the passer can step and throw in the direction desired. The old, but still valid theory—that if either the passer or receiver is stationary, the chances for completions are increased—is supportive of the drop-back technique.

A third factor for consideration in the drop-back pass is that of time allotment. There is no question that this phase of passing will allow the thrower more time to pass. Because the ball is thrown from the middle and directly behind the offensive line, with blockers on both sides of the passer, there is a secure atmosphere present. It is felt that this walled area established by the design of the play is difficult to penetrate.

Coaching points

Basing the drop-back pass upon fundamental specifics is as important as any other aspect of football. When teaching the drop-back pass technique, there are some hints which help a passer better establish his mastery of the skill. Daily practice of these aspects will aid in their perfection. Coaches must, therefore, maintain close supervision and check to see that the quarterback correctly performs the following:

1) Receives laces properly.
2) Brings ball up to body.
3) Sets up correctly.
4) Grips ball properly.
5) Gets ball over head.
6) Gets nose of ball up.
7) Keeps wrist straight.
8) Points body in right direction.
9) Follows through with pass.
10) Observes patterns being run and defensive rush.
11) Sets up fast enough.
12) Releases ball at proper time in relation to pattern being run.

DROP-BACK QUARTERBACK TECHNIQUES

There are some specific quarterback techniques, in carrying out drop-back action, which determine precision of procedure. As in any other phase of football, execution is dependent upon sound methodology. Listed below are the intricate maneuvers of the quarterback relative to the drop-back pass.

1) Stance
   A. Feet should be spread about hip wide or slightly more.
   B. Hips should be in a comfortable position parallel to line of scrimmage or one foot back slightly.
   C. Knees should be bent to a comfortable angle.
   D. Body should be at a forward angle with shoulders rounded and hips about even with line of scrimmage, close to Center.

2) Hand position of quarterback

    A. Passing hand should be up and other hand down so that the hands form a "V".

    B. Distance from center and position of hands should be directed by bending arms and keeping elbows near body.

    C. Quarterback's fingers must be spread and extended while at the same time relaxed.

    D. Upper hand placed firmly against center's crotch to provide target.

3) Center-quarterback exchange

    A. Starts with ball being placed in proper position by Center so that it strikes quarterback's hands solidly, with laces of ball hitting fingers of upper hand.

    B. Quarterback covers ball with lower hand and begins play-action.

4) Follow-through

    A. Quarterback must ride center a little with hands and arms to prevent poor exchange due to timing.

5) Ready to throw

    A. Bring ball to body about stomach high.

    B. Adjust ball for passing by getting laces set across fingers.

    C. Shoulders rounded in to hide ball as much as possible.

6) The set-up

    A. Drives off one foot and lead steps with other.

    B. Head and shoulders should be ahead of body.

    C. Bring ball up from stomach to shoulder height while planting back foot to set up.

    D. Distance of drop-back sprint is generally 5, 7, or 9 yards depending upon depth of pass to be thrown.

    E. Body should drive off back foot while hips turn in direction of line of scrimmage.

    F. Weight of body must be evenly distributed to establish a proper balance.

    G. Back knee should then bend slightly and back shoulder drops.

H. Point front in direction pass will be released.

I. Bend back knee and drop back shoulder to ready for arm swing back.

J. Bring ball to a point necessary to ready the forward movement of arm. (This would depend on distance ball will be thrown.)

K. Allow arm to come forward, keep elbow bent by wrist straining in direction of receiver.

L. Bring fingers toward front and release ball with fingers following.

Though we promote the above basics for quarterbacks, some of the greatest passers in the game violate these rules. (It must be remembered that only the great can *afford* to neglect fundamentals.) Sound rules are imperative to most players and teams; execution of any phase of the game is founded upon fundamentals. If the aforementioned procedures are adhered to, the result will be a passer that is mechanically sound. Though fundamentals be but a phase of passing, nonetheless they rank high in importance and should not be taken lightly.

MENTAL COMPETENCE

Once a passer has correctly set up and readied to pass, the real test of this type of passing begins. Here is where poise and alertness play an important role. As he locates his receiver the passer must zero in on target, while all the time the wall is closing in on him. After sighting the location of the receiver, a decision must be made as to whether to throw or not. This decision is split-second, and yet there is no room for error! The ball must leave on time and arrive according to schedule. Only accuracy and timing here will lead to a completion.

In the drop-back technique of passing there is reason and need to establish proper timing. Timing concerns itself with setting up in the pocket and getting the ball to the receiver on time and target. Elementary though this may seem, it can be a problem if not done properly. A common and effective method that helps the timing of the quarterback's drop-back maneuver is to use the *count system.*

The count system involves the quarterback's setting up according to the type of pass being thrown. If the pattern run is short in nature, the passer sets up on the third step, while his receiver counts three and looks for the ball. Accordingly, a five-count action would be a deeper pattern wherein the passer and receiver count to five before the ball is released or looked for.

The advantage of the count system is that the timing of the play is always correct. The receiver is at the right place at the right time, while the quarterback is delivering the pigskin on schedule.

"THE WALL IS ALL"

The game of football is based upon teamwork. If any phase of teamwork breaks down, so goes success. A drop-back action pass is based upon a sustaining kind of protection. There can be no leaks, no missed assignments—only long, hard continued blocking!

Usually, the breakdown of protection is due to pressure from linebackers or interior linemen. The immediate rush comes between tackles, although a secondary rush will come from the outside. Thus any drop-back passing team must be able to, first, take the wave of interior people and, then, ward off exterior pressure. (Specific blocking techniques are discussed in the chapter on pass protection blocking. Pass protection blocking is mentioned here only to stress its importance to the drop-back pass and the connection between it and drop-back passing.)

What is pertinent here is that a drop-back team must have a quarterback who can read pressure and determine when to react to it and when not. If the inside rush is great, a passer has to be able to run out of the protection; if pressure is outside, the quarterback must step up and throw from inside the pressure. In short, a good drop-back passer has to be able to read and react, as well as pass. Knowing *when* to pass or run is as important as knowing *how* to throw.

POSITION OF QUARTERBACK'S BODY

A very controversial subject is the position of the passer's body while dropping back and setting up. We deliberately did not discuss this concept earlier, as part of the quarterback techniques, because there are many ways to accomplish properly dropping back. The two methods are the *back-peddle* and the *sprint-back*.

Back-peddle

This style involves the quarterback taking the exchange and dropping straight back as fast as possible. Supporters of this type of action believe that back-peddling allows the passer greater vision, in that the field of play is always in front of him. This procedure eliminates losing the receiver during the early stages of play. It also provides the quarterback with a good look at the defensive secondary. A disadvantage of the back-peddle technique is that it creates loss of deception, since the ball can be seen throughout the entire setting-up procedure.

Sprint-back

The sprint-back type of drop-back action is sound, in that the passer can reach the throwing position sooner through this technique. This type of passing makes the quarterback "open step" with one foot or another and sprint straight back to a throwing position. The negative aspect here is that the passer does not see the field of play during the entire dropping-back period.

Both methods are sound and functionable. The criteria for determining which kind of drop-back action to use should be based on the coach's philosophy and the type of personnel available. Over the years it has been our experience that the best way to decide on the particular drop-back method is to help the quarterback perfect what seems most natural to him. Many of the better passers use a combination of the two techniques. By sprinting back and looking upfield at the same time, it is possible to set up swiftly and yet retain a good view of the field. Regardless of the technique, the drop-back pass has, without question, a place in every offense. Realize it—believe it—accept it!

6

How to Prevent
Pressure Defenses

Almost everyone agrees that the best pass defense is a good rush on a passer. If this be so, then the way to produce successful passing is to prevent defensive pressure. Proper protection is the first step toward completing passes. The numerous types of pass protection utilized today generally can be classified into two categories: the *man-for-man* and *pure cup* protection. The following pages represent an attempt to combine these methods of protection.

KEEPING THE LANE OPEN

We have labeled the real estate inside the *wall of protection* (see Figure 6-1) as the "standoff zone," the buffer blocking zone for interior linemen. In this area, the standoff between the protectors and defenders is made. This is the place where some penetration is allowed, but position on opponent and maintaining balance are crucial. Going to the ground or permitting penetration inside this interior-linemen blocking zone may hamper the success of a pass.

A zone or area that needs discussion is the "inside perimeter." Located 2½ yards behind the line of scrimmage and ex-

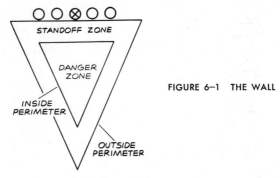

FIGURE 6–1   THE WALL

tending to the outside shoulder of offensive tackles, this zone continues from the outside shoulder of the tackles, backward at an angle to a point 9 yards behind offensive center. This zone within the inside perimeter is the passing lane, and we refer to it as the danger zone. All defensive people must be kept out of this lane until the pass is released. If this is not done, the defense has succeeded in applying pressure on the quarterback.

The "outside perimeter" is formed approximately 2½ yards outside of the inside perimeter. This line of defense makes up the points at which the original contact with the enemy is made, as well as the place from which the wall of protection begins. The deepest point of the perimeter is where the quarterback makes his initial set after sprinting back to throw.

As stated earlier, the area between the two offensive guards (in a balanced line) and approximately 9 yards deep is called the passing lane. Any passing attack depends on maintaining an open lane from which the passer can throw. When defensive players penetrate this area, pressure on the passer is the result. The function of pass protection is to keep the enemy out of this critical real estate. Responsibility for defending the lane is shared between the interior linemen and the blocking backs. There are many ways to accomplish this feat. Let's first consider the job of the interior linemen.

There are three basic types of pass protection blocking for linemen. They are the drop-step, fire-out, and combination. It is agreed that all techniques have their merits; however, the drop step has many important advantages.

DROP-STEP TECHNIQUE

Linemen should, from their three-point stance, take a short drop-step (no more than 6 inches) with the outside foot. As the outside foot drops back, arms should come up chest high to catch the force of defensive linemen. Feet should immediately begin moving up and down like pistons to maintain balance and help the blocker keep proper position on his defensive man. A blocker should give ground as he maintains his block, but territory should be given grudgingly. Offensive linemen should always keep in mind they are giving ground for time, and that time gained will allow the pass to be thrown.

EFFECTIVE PASS PROTECTION BLOCKING TECHNIQUES

The function of pass protectors is, generally speaking, threefold: the hitting, extending, and recovery aspects. In each of these phases of blocking, it is position of feet that makes the difference. If feet are permitted to get too close together or be crossed, slowing down penetration will be impossible. A well-balanced stance, with weight evenly distributed, will bring about effective blocking.

Considering the hitting stage of blocking, it is essential that legs be under the body in a supporting position. Knees are bent, hips are parallel and extended forward slightly on making contact. Weight is principally on the balls of the feet and is shifted from the feet through the knees and hips to the chest, head, and forearms. As contact is made, the blocker begins the second phase of protection.

Extension of the blocker's body involves the follow-through portion of pass protection. After a hit is made the forearms, shoulders, and head must be brought up into the rusher to slow his charge. While in this state, the body is completely uncoiled since the knees, hips, and back have been straightened.

The neck is in a bulled state; the head is back while the chest and arms are out and up. With weight being distributed so far forward, the extension phase of protection must be quickly followed by body recovery.

During recovery, legs must again be brought under the body to insure balance and position on the opponent. Recovery begins as an extension of the body is made by bringing the legs up to a hitting position as soon as the final stage of contact is made. As the forearms rip and lift the opposition, the legs should begin their movement forward, thus concluding the cycle of the pass block. The previously mentioned blocking technique can be referred to as control pass protection blocking.

Pass protection blocking must never allow anyone to penetrate to the inside. The main reason for drop-stepping is to invite defensive linemen to rush from the outside. Encouraging them to charge from the outside provides the offense with extra time. Keeping the enemy out of the wall in turn permits the passer to operate successfully within this arc of protection.

A passer can help his cause and the job of pass protection by setting up to throw correctly. (The passers' drop-back technique is described in another chapter.) Briefly, however, it should be pointed out that a passer who sets too deeply allows the outside rush to get to him and places the pass protection blockers in an unfavorable position. When the passer does not drop back deep enough, he becomes vulnerable to pressure and forces interior linemen to sustain their blocks longer. While there are many theories on correct depth for passers to set up, we feel that a distance of 9 yards can best aid those who are forming the protective wall or cup.

Much time must be spent developing correct techniques if pass protection blocking is to be consistently effective. Players themselves must believe in their team's ability to throw the football. They must accept the concept that the success of every pass completion depends upon pass protection. If linemen absorb this idea, development of proper techniques and fundamentals will follow.

Fundamental lineman techniques

1) Arms high.
2) Knees bent, and try never to completely uncoil at knees.
3) Head in chin of defensive man.
4) Weight on balls of feet.
5) Eyes open at all times.
6) Keep position on opponent by maintaining body between him and passer.
7) Move feet, short choppy steps.
8) Chest and shoulders fire up and into chest of opposition, block through defense.
9) Stay on feet if at all possible!

Blocking blitzing linebackers

Another aspect of pass protection blocking that is often neglected is red-dogging linebackers. One of the real challenges faced by the passing game is the big rush linebackers can provide. This pressure often comes quicker, is unexpected, and is more effective than the normal defensive lineman rush. Picking up and blocking these linebackers when they fire is a must in order for the passer to get the ball off.

There are many ways or rules that can be adopted to cut off these linebackers. One of the better techniques is to teach the blocking area method. This technique involves offensive linemen from tackle to tackle simply blocking shoulder to shoulder, closing down on any rush that might occur (see Figure 6-2).

FIGURE 6–2   AREA BLOCKING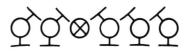

Always block gap to inside first if it is threatened.

Man-for-man protection

Another way to pick up these dogging linebackers and also a sound method of protection is the count-off system. By counting from the inside out, offensive linemen can each be responsible for a given defensive man. This establishes the responsibility of blocking a given linebacker or lineman, to a specific person. This rule is simple and adaptable to any defense a team might see. Have offensive guards block the first man on or off the line of scrimmage, outside the offensive center. Tackles block the second man on or off the line of scrimmage outside of center. When using this method of pass blocking, defensive linebackers are counted off as if they are linemen (see Figure 6-3). The basic principle in establishing this form of protection is that each pass blocker blocks his assigned man regardless of where he goes. The backs block the first man outside the block of the tackle. If an end is used to block, he blocks the third man on or off the line of scrimmage outside of center. The back then blocks the first man outside the block of the end.

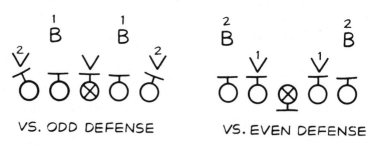

VS. ODD DEFENSE

VS. EVEN DEFENSE

On even defense, center area blocks.

FIGURE 6–3   COUNT-OFF METHOD

BACKFIELD PROTECTION

Normally in a "T" formation offense, two backs will pass block to supplement the blocking of the line. This is referred to as normal protection, as shown in Figure 6-4. This usually is an outside type of protection, with halfbacks block-

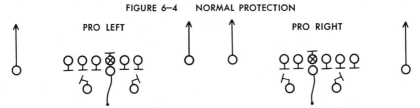

FIGURE 6–4   NORMAL PROTECTION

In using normal protection the backs block the first man outside block of tackles or tight end if he is not utilized in pattern.

ing outside the rush of the defenders. When halfbacks are called on to pass block, their rules for blocking are somewhat different than that of linemen. Backs are smaller and in many cases unable to handle bigger defensive ends. Therefore halfbacks should take their first step up and then face outside to take on the defender. This enables the halfback to block the end at an inside-out angle rather than a straight-ahead approach. The second phase of pass blocking is to block with a reverse shoulder whenever possible. This again allows the blocker an edge since he does not have to take big guys head-on. A reverse shoulder block on the opposition should force the rusher behind and outside of the passer—that is, if the passer has stepped up into the lane correctly.

There are times, naturally, when two backs are needed in a pass pattern. This type of pass play generally is of a flood nature. The most effective way to release two backs into a pattern and still get good solid protection is to keep an end home to block. This type of protection generally lends itself to the shorter pass. You can accomplish this by blocking with the end opposite the direction of the flow of backs (see Figure 6-5).

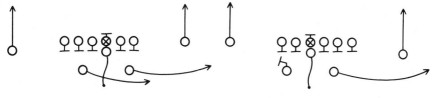

FLOOD PATTERN   NORMAL COMBINATION PROTECTION

FIGURE 6–5   COMBINATION PROTECTION

One combination method of protection uses a back to block to the outside and an end to the other. Another common way to pass protect is to pull an uncovered lineman to block to the outside while a remaining back blocks to the other side.

INTERIOR LINEMEN BLOCKING DEFENSIVE ENDS

Pulling interior linemen to block defensive ends is another method proven effective. This style of protection helps the offense in a number of ways. It places a bigger, stronger lineman in the position of blocking a rugged end, instead of a small, less qualified back. When a lineman pulls to take on an end, it generally allows a back to be used in a pattern. This maneuver enables the offense to be much more flexible in the play pattern selection and use of appropriate receivers.

A sound, simple rule to determine who pulls out of line to block ends and when this should take place is: The guard, tackle, or center uncovered by a defensive lineman will pull to the call side. If, for example, the call is to the right side of the offense, the uncovered lineman will pull to that side.

The only exception to this law would be when the "uncovered" lineman is covered by a linebacker who looks as if he might blitz. On this occasion the lineman would pass block in a normal manner. The back then generally assigned to block the end would carry out his task. There are numerous signals that can be used to transmit this blocking change. The technique we use is to have the uncovered lineman place one hand on his hip as a sign to the back that he will not be pulling out of line to block the end. This message is conveyed at the

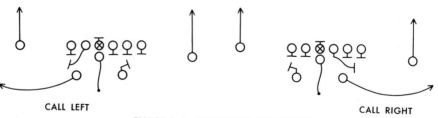

CALL LEFT   CALL RIGHT

FIGURE 6–6   UNCOVERED PROTECTION

line of scrimmage just prior to the beginning of the cadence (see Figure 6-6).

It is believed that the foregoing is a sound method that will provide a team with an effective form of protection. This theory can be used on all levels of competition. It is simple yet flexible enough to handle any defensive system employed.

PSYCHOLOGICAL ASPECTS OF PASS PROTECTION

If linemen are going to withstand the strain of onrushing linemen play after play, they must be convinced that their efforts are going to win the contest. Instilling and maintaining this confidence is a never-ending task. Coaches have to continually sell the footballers. Making believers out of these people is done primarily through a psychological approach.

We like to first tell our pass protectors that they are the backbone of the aerial attack and *on their shoulders rests our passing game.* To emphasize this, awards are made each week, to interior linemen, based on number of completions in the previous game. A pen and pencil set goes to all pass protectors if the team gains 200 yards passing. When the club scores two touchdowns or more through the air in a given game, each player is awarded a plaque. Trophies are given at the end of the season if 2,000 yards or twenty touchdowns are acquired. Financing these gifts is a good project for the local Boosters' Club or letterman's association.

To further establish the importance of pass protectors, a special name can be given this select group. A label such as "The Hard-Nosed Group" is quite appropriate and tends to encourage pride and stature. A bulletin board can be used that is titled "The Hard-Nosed Group In Action," with photos of their efforts in last week's game.

Still another device that can highlight the job of pass blockers is to give each member of the group an identifying symbol. Insignias on helmets, stripes on sleeves, a different type or color of face mask or bar may well accomplish the objective.

What is important is that there is identification—that these young men stand out.

Newspapers, radio, and other means of communication can also play a large role in projecting the aforementioned image. Being given credit for a job well done, in the paper or on the radio, has tremendous impact upon everyone. Special praise in a rally, or even in front of the squad, will have a positive effect. These and other such methods help develop the psychological edge needed by every team.

PASS BLOCKING MUST BE REALISTIC TO BE DEVELOPED

Unless pass protection blocking is practiced realistically, it will break down when it is time to play. Realism fosters learning. If the pass protection is expected to hold five seconds, then this amount of time should be worked toward in all forms of pass protection drills. In fact, expect more than the minimum amount in practice. *This is realistic!*

Since opposition each week will be other human beings, it is only rational that preparation for this war involve live work. So often we coaches are guilty of putting bags, sleds, or other mechanical apparatus in front of our kids all week and then expecting them to do the job on game day. Most of these teaching aids are not realistic because they do not move or hit back. There is no substitute for a warm body. Blocking live in practice is probably more important in pass blocking than in any other phase of blocking. The bigger, tougher, and faster the individual, the better the experience for the pass protectors. *This is realistic!*

By placing a greater number of defensive people opposite offensive players, a more game-like condition prevails. It is far more sensible to be prepared for the worst and have the routine occur, than to be ready for normal situations when the abnormal situation develops. By working against numerous defenders, blockers are required to think, react, and execute their assignments under the poorest possible conditions. To complicate matters even more, linebackers should be placed in blitzing positions and asked to red-dog as pass blockers pick them up. This technique is called the Overload Principle. Players who can handle blocking assignments such as just stated have little trouble come game time. *This is realistic!*

SOMETHING TO REMEMBER

Hit, hit, hit again! The result—time! Men who act as the shield for the passer and allow him time to throw, are the *hitters*. Winning depends upon their courage and intestinal fortitude. They take bruises and lumps to gain a little precious time. In essence, these footballers are the pulse and backbone of an aerial attack. Those close to the game know that pass protectors determine success or failure for every pass thrown, in every game played. Without pass protection, there is no passing game!

7

Coaching Multiple
Pass Patterns—
The Simple Way

Multiplicity plus simplicity in pass patterns leads to effective passing. To instill these features in your offense, a combination of numbers and names to describe passing plays is used. This technique indicates the side of the field to which the ball will be passed, types of patterns to be run, prime receiver, and formation and action of play from which the pass will be thrown. If need be, allowance can also be made for the man-in-motion. In short, this method is flawless in nature and extremely elementary.

NUMBERS DIVIDE THE OFFENSE

By dividing your pass offense into a right and left side, those who run the patterns can be identified better. Right side of the offense can be termed "80", while the left is called "90". In calling a pattern, if the toss is going to be to the right side, it's an 80 pass. On the other hand, if the ball is thrown to the left side, it's a 90 pass. Receivers located on the left side of the ball normally concern themselves with 90 call patterns, while those on the right are involved in 80 call routes.

NAMING THE RECEIVERS

To add further simplicity to calling pass patterns, names can be given the backs. What names are assigned specific backs is a matter for each coach to decide. Names used for our receivers are *Lou, Rip,* and *Fred.* Full realization of the effectiveness of using names to identify receivers is relevant when a specific individual pattern is called. For example, a pass pattern could be, "90, Rip look-in." This descriptive call states that the play will be to the left side, Rip is the receiver, and the pattern is a look-in. Another advantage to naming the backs is discussed later in this chapter when the man-in-motion is described.

DESCRIBING THE PATTERNS

As previously stated, labeling patterns helps to identify them. This is especially true when names assigned to routes clearly describe them. The description of patterns identifies the individual, two-man, multiple, and special courses by the direction and type of route taken. The first pattern mentioned when a play is called is the course of the prime receiver, while the next calls the direct secondary receivers.

INDIVIDUAL ROUTES

The single-man pass pattern is the basis for the entire passing game. Perfection in execution of fundamental patterns is a must. Actually, pass receiving comes down to one man beating another on a given play. Single patterns are easy to call because only one man is involved. Like all patterns outlined in this chapter, individual routes are named to describe the pattern run. Individual routes are *look-in, post, curl, flag, hook,*

hook-go, square-in, square-out, and *out-up.* Most of these patterns are shown in Figure 7-1.

Regardless of the type of pass play, each receiver performs his own specific maneuver. When more than one individual patterns are put together, the result is combination patterns. Combination courses include two-man patterns, multiple routes, and special passes.

Two-man patterns

Two-man patterns utilize two men in the pattern, each running separate routes. Generally, one pattern complements the other. Two-man routes are particularly good against a zone defensive secondary. This form of pattern, like the in-

FIGURE 7–1 INDIVIDUAL ROUTES

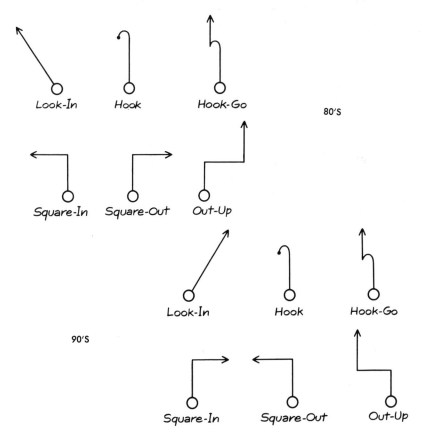

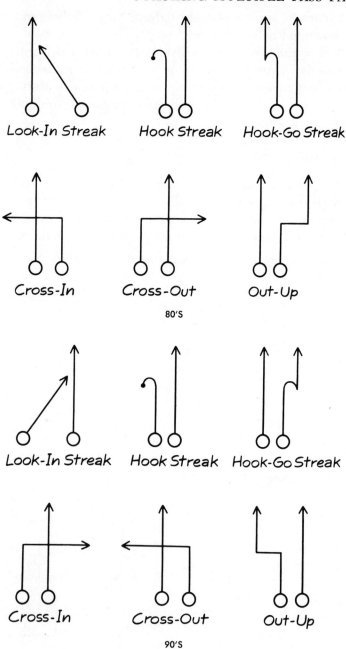

FIGURE 7–2　TWO-MAN PATTERNS

dividual type, is descriptive in essence. Some very effective two-man patterns are *look-in streak, hook-streak, hook-go, cross-in, cross-out,* and *out-up streak.* Figure 7-2 exhibits each of these two-man patterns.

The two-man pattern often forces a defensive man to make a decision or choose between two receivers running routes in his area. Any time a defense is required to make judgments the offense has established an advantage. Judgments lead to mistakes.

It should be pointed out that two-man courses are perhaps the most common form of pass patterns used. They may involve two receivers on the same side of scrimmage running complementary patterns, or receivers from both sides of the offense sprinting separate routes.

MULTIPLE COURSES

Multiple pass patterns refer to plays that have three or more receivers. Routes using this number of players permit a given defensive zone to be flooded with more receivers than defenders. To maintain continuity and simplicity, descriptive terms are used to describe play. Multiple pass pattern plays are *cut-break swing, Zorro-curl swing, curl-flag swing, hook-cross swing, post-curl swing, out swing, cross-out swing,* and *cross-in swing.* Multiple courses are shown in Figures 7-3 to 7-6.

Drop-back action is particularly effective in executing the multiple pass pattern approach. Since this kind of pattern generally takes an extended length of time to execute, it is ideal to throw here from the drop-back style which provides for the best possible protection and increases the probability of succeeding.

The benefit of multiple courses is that they feature many receivers in each play from which to select. Logically, the more pass catchers involved, the greater the chance for one being open. A multitude of individual moves increases the difficulty of defending effectively.

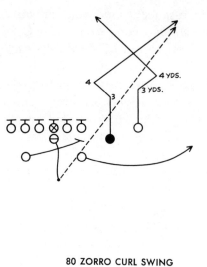

80 CUT BREAK SWING

80 ZORRO CURL SWING

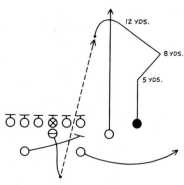

FIGURE 7–3

FIGURE 7–4

80 HOOK CROSS SWING

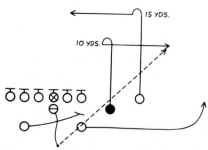

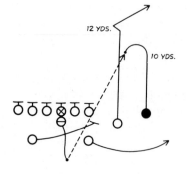

80 CURL FLAG SWING

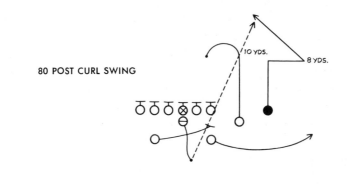

80 POST CURL SWING

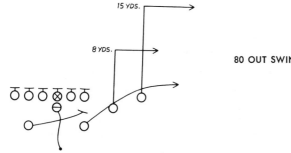

80 OUT SWING

FIGURE 7–5

FIGURE 7–6

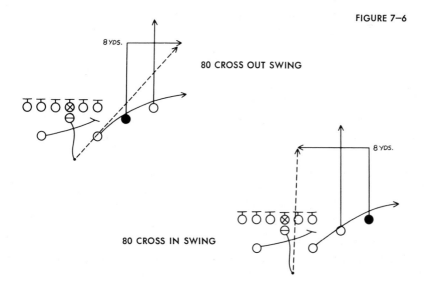

80 CROSS OUT SWING

80 CROSS IN SWING

The only real disadvantage of multiple route patterns is that they tend to limit play-action to the drop-back approach, and long-sustaining protection normally has to be maintained. This should not be construed to mean that multiple patterns cannot be run from other play-actions or that short passes cannot result from multiple courses. Chapters 9 and 11, which deal with the sprint-out and play-action plays, point out some of the other possibilities of multiple pass patterns.

"OVER CALL"

Pass patterns can be strengthened by occasionally combining receivers from both sides of the offense. The "over call" provides the end from the side away from the play to run a course just behind the linebackers into the pattern area. The term "over" directs a pass catcher, ordinarily not in the pattern, to become a secondary receiver. These "over calls" allow crossing patterns, as well as help place an additional man in the flood course. In short, the man running the "over" route supplies a safety valve for any pattern called. Examples of "over calls" are shown in Figures 7-7 to 7-9.

To include an "over call" as part of a regular pass play might involve individual, two-man, or multiple patterns *and* the "over call." This would combine an established pattern and an additional receiver from the off side. Flexibility provided by this type of pass pattern structure is unlimited in its potential. The magnitude of possible patterns when using the "over call" is restricted only by the desirability of play. However, there may be times when an added receiver would do more harm than good in a given pattern, since he could encourage abnormal coverage or interfere with prime receivers in his route.

Using the "over" pattern as part of a pass play should be employed sparingly when the defense is placing a great deal of pressure on passer. If your aerial attack is hampered by a strong rush, it is advisable to keep the end at home to aid in protecting the passer. A good rule for determining when an end is to

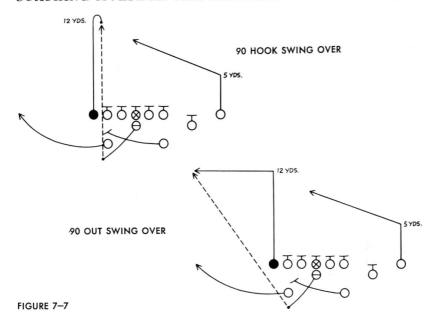

FIGURE 7–7

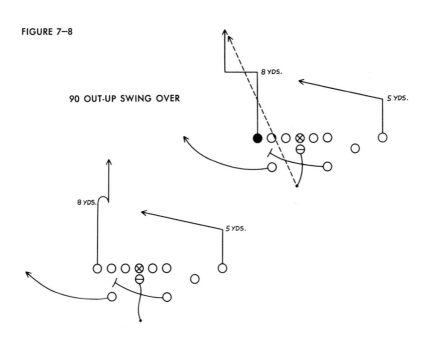

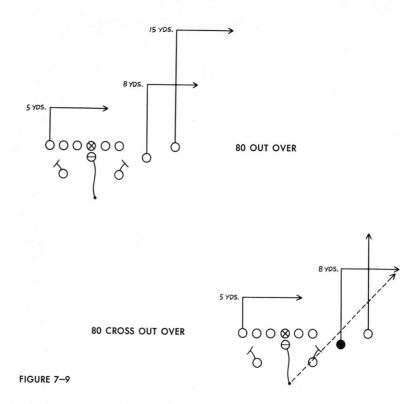

FIGURE 7–9

release or to remain is: *If seven or more of the opposition line up on the line of scrimmage, the end does not release.* The end himself can read this and resolve his assignment according to his defense.

SPECIAL PATTERNS

In every offense there are certain plays that are difficult to classify in terms of description. They are plays that overlap the normal methodology of pattern calling. These special plays, however, often adhere to other descriptive names that make identity easy. Special patterns are presented in Figures 7-10 to 7-13 and include *split, sneak,* and *banana.*

MOTION IN PATTERN

Though the man-in-motion has been briefly described already, we will discuss it in connection with pass patterns. Motion can be of aid to a receiver in the passing game through the use of short and long motion. A receiver can be placed in motion for a short duration or an extended course, depending on the pattern to be run. Thus, basic patterns can be strengthened by long or short motion.

When a man is placed in motion, he runs an automatic swing-type pattern to the call side. Which back goes in motion is determined when his name is added to the play called. Again, this is one reason for naming backs. A play might be "90 out *Rip,*" or a pass to the left end running an out-pattern, with the back named Mac in motion. (In our offense, Rip is our slotback.) It should be emphasized that any back can be put in motion by simply stating his chosen football name after the play and pattern have been called.

If the name of the back is followed by the term "away," the back would run motion away from the call side. This destroys any key that might be established in relation to motion always going to the call side. An away call can help keep a defense honest when it is overcompensating to motion, as well as providing balance to a pass offense.

DOUBLE YOUR PASS PATTERNS—FLIP-FLOP

If identical patterns and plays can be run to both sides with the same personnel, an offense has twice its original potential. Widely known as flip-flopping, this increases the threat of every play by permitting the best-suited players to be in the most desired positions at all times. Thus the split end is always

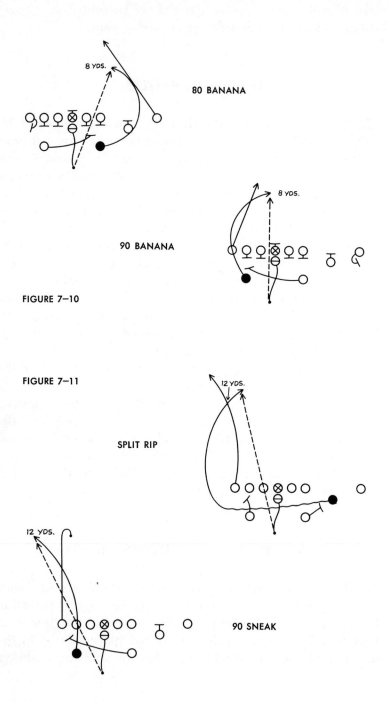

80 BANANA

90 BANANA

FIGURE 7–10

FIGURE 7–11

SPLIT RIP

90 SNEAK

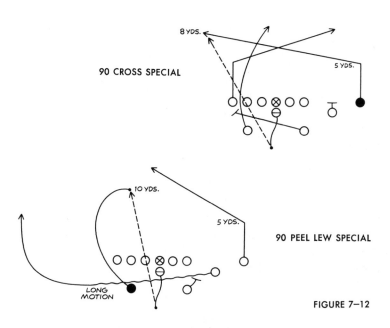

90 CROSS SPECIAL

90 PEEL LEW SPECIAL

FIGURE 7–12

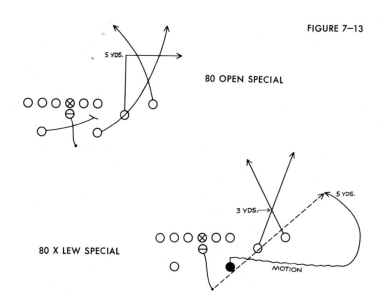

FIGURE 7–13

80 OPEN SPECIAL

80 X LEW SPECIAL

a split end, the tight end a tight end, and so forth, so that more specialization results.

By providing your pass offense with numbers and names as indicated previously, flip-flopping becomes a reality. Patterns that complement the slot or flanker side are referred to as 80 patterns, while those to the weak side are 90 routes. By simply adding the letter L or R prior to the 80 or 90 call, the same courses can be run to either side. An *R* 80 cross-out play would be a pattern to the right side, while *L* 80 is the exact play with the same personnel executing to left side.

All patterns presented in this chapter can be run to either side of the offense. Flip-flopping not only increases the number of patterns, but simplifies them by permitting specialists in every position to perfect their basic assignments. Lastly, turning the offense over can provide better field position for a particular pattern and easily place the best offensive people against the weakest defensive men.

PASS PATTERN DEVIATIONS

A major problem facing your offense is irregular defensive alignments. It is not difficult to defeat a standard defensive set with one or another pass pattern. Obviously, all defensive sets have their weaknesses. And furthermore, each form of coverage within the defensive formation has its vulnerability. When a linebacker is forced to cover a halfback or an end, and still defend the fullback run, the defense is placed at a disadvantage.

Because many defenses today are structured around abnormal alignments and odd-ball forms of coverage, an offense must compensate and defeat these maneuvers by striking at the soft spots in these variations. To overcome defensive alignments and exploit defensive weaknesses, the pass offense must be flexible to the extent of changing or modifying some phases of play, specifically pass patterns.

Most coaches teach specific pass routes receivers should run. This is, of course, necessary in any passing offense. However, we feel that receivers must be able to run the basic patterns of our offense and, in addition, be able to deviate from the set route if necessary. Need for deviation from the basic pattern can be caused by deployment of the secondary, field position, down and distance to go, and ability of offensive and defensive personnel.

Some defensive sets are designed to defend against the bomb, while others play to take away the sprint-out or roll-out pass. Many defensive secondaries concentrate on covering the key receiver well, or taking away the offense's best pass pattern. Regardless of what the defensive secondary is attempting to do, receivers must be able to make adjustments and free themselves from their opposition.

Moves that allow patterns to be shortened or lengthened can be employed. (Specific moves are discussed on Chapter 3.) An example of a deviation might be for a receiver to run his sideline or square-out pattern at eight yards instead of twelve, if the secondary is conscious of the deep pattern.

Field position is another cause for deviation, since some defensive secondaries like to defend the wide side of the field. A receiver must be able to alter his route when running a pattern to the wide side. For example, he might run a down-and-back pattern rather than a down-and-out; he might choose a hook instead of a curl pattern.

Closely associated with defensive secondary alignment and field position, as reasons for deviation from basic pass patterns, is down and distance. These dictate the depth a specific pattern will be run. Generally speaking, a pattern should be run deep enough to gain the necessary yardage for a first down. This is particularly true on third or fourth down, since passing attempts become *musts* if the drive is to continue.

A final deviation a receiver might need to consider has to do with the ability of the receiver and that of the defender. If, for example, the receiver is slow and the defender fast, the only way the offensive man can defeat the defensive man is to beat him with a fake or move. However, if the offensive man has more speed than his opponent, he might simply make a cut and outrun the defender. Thus, the individual's abilities determine how the pattern will be run.

SPLIT END CALL

When using individual patterns, it is helpful to allow the split end the option of changing the pattern at the line of scrimmage. Our experience has shown that defensive position placement can help or hinder given patterns. A receiver who lines up in an unfavorable position in relation to the defender may, by calling a different pattern, have success.

There are four basic, individual patterns that compensate for any position placement a secondaryman might assume. These patterns are look-in, out, hook, and streak. If a defender lines up to the outside of a receiver, a look-in route can be called, while if he is to the inside, an out pattern might be best. A defensive man set ten yards deep may encourage a look course, just as a defender lined up five or six yards could stimulate a streak pattern call.

Signals used to make this call are extremely simple. The split end puts the hand nearest the quarterback on his near hip if look-in is called. An out pattern is transmitted to the quarterback by placing a hand farthest from ball on his waist. The hook route is signaled by placing both hands on hips. A streak pattern is declared when the receiver puts one hand behind his back. All calls are made at the line of scrimmage as soon as the receiver reaches his starting position. Only the quarterback and split end need be concerned with this procedure. Linemen and other personnel should carry out their assignments as they were originally called.

KEEP IN MIND

Pass patterns fall into two classifications—short and long. A sound passing attack needs courses of a deep nature as well as the shallow type. A throwing attack has but limited value if an offense exemplifies only one of these potentials.

Short patterns are designed to defeat linebackers first and the secondary next. Patterns considered short are no more than fifteen yards deep. When linebackers are held by good faking and ball handling, they cannot stop a pass in the ten-to-fifteen yard deep area. This means that the secondary must defend against this pattern. It is unlikely that secondarymen can successfully and constantly prevent completions in this zone. Hooks, square-ins, hook-crosses, and cross-ins can all be run effectively off some form of backfield action. Short patterns are attempts to throw the ball in front of deep backs and behind linebackers.

Deeper patterns function to force one man to cover another for an extended period of time. All things being equal, the better man will win. If and when a deeper pattern can be successfully executed, the offense has broken defensive containment, which can lead to real trouble. It goes without saying that just a few deep completions will win the game.

SO MUCH FOR MULTIPLICITY AND SIMPLICITY

By using both numbers and descriptive terms, many pass patterns can be learned easily without resorting to memorizing numbers or letters. Using the aforementioned method of pattern calling, a footballer can acquire in a day his offense's entire group of pass patterns. It's simple—it's sound—it's successful!

8

Supplementing the
Passing Game

In football there are some things you can't do, others you can do, and others you *must* do. Certain plays are known and accepted as basic and sound. Whether you can't, can, or must use these plays is determined by the type of passing action used. Therefore, a team that utilizes the drop-back pass not only benefits from this kind of pass, but provides for related plays by the action of the play. These plays can become an intrinsic part of an offense.

WHAT MAKES RELATED PLAYS GO?

All of the following plays associated with the drop-back pass depend upon throwing as an important part of the offense if they are to function.

The safety valve

In a drop-back attack it is imperative that a safety valve pass be installed. A back swings out of the backfield and becomes a secondary receiver. This play is employed when the defense puts an overloaded rush on one side of the offense, to "burn" a blitzing linebacker, or to provide a receiver when the primary receiver is covered.

The safety valve pass can be predetermined or developed as a result of a big rush from the defense. When the safety valve is predetermined, the halfback usually runs the flare-action pattern to the side of the pass play called. On a play call to the split end, the safety valve would swing to that side. If the call was to the tight end, the safety valve would then swing to that side. When the predetermined call is made, the quarterback can direct the safety valve by simply saying "swing" as the play is being called in the huddle. An example might be "80 cross-out *swing.*" A cross-out route is then run, and the back set to the call side would run the swing or act as the safety valve.

Another form of safety valve is not predetermined. This second type becomes an automatic pattern when the defense overloads the play call side and places the offense in a disadvantageous position. When a pattern is called to one end or the other and the remaining back set to that side is released into the pattern, it is difficult to effectively block this play call side if an overload occurs. Thus the safety valve will run a swing action to the call side if this situation presents itself. The back himself determines the feasibility of running the safety valve pattern.

The screen pass

One of the biggest plays in football, this is one of the few passing plays that can be run from practically any field position. It differs from others in that the major concerns are no longer pass protection, the running of proper patterns, and throwing the strike. Concentration is on timing and deception. Regardless of the type of screen being run (see Figures 8-1 to 8-6), it is important to prevent the defense from knowing it to be a screen for the longest possible time. It is likewise important to throw the pass when the offensive line has set up properly, the receiver is in position, and the defense is in the worst possible position to defend against it.

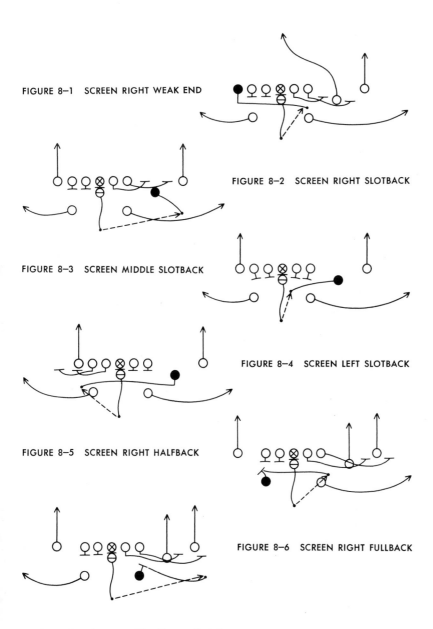

FIGURE 8–1   SCREEN RIGHT WEAK END

FIGURE 8–2   SCREEN RIGHT SLOTBACK

FIGURE 8–3   SCREEN MIDDLE SLOTBACK

FIGURE 8–4   SCREEN LEFT SLOTBACK

FIGURE 8–5   SCREEN RIGHT HALFBACK

FIGURE 8–6   SCREEN RIGHT FULLBACK

1) The weak end can vary his splits on all of these screens.
2) On any of these screens, one of the backs can be placed in motion by adding the back's assigned name as described in a previous chapter.

Generally a screen is more effective when thrown to the wide side of the field—but not always. The side to which the screen is thrown should be determined by offensive and defensive personnel, as well as by down and distance. Certainly a screen should be thrown to one of the better open-field running backs on the club, and if possible, be thrown on first or second down.

We have found that a screen pass will have a better chance of succeeding if certain factors prevail. These factors are:

1) Receiver is in a standing position facing passer when ball is thrown.

2) Passer does not look in direction of screen when setting up to throw.

3) Offensive line blocks for at least two counts before releasing to form screen.

4) There is a man-in-motion away from screen or a flanker set to opposite side of screen pattern.

5) Passer sets up physically as quickly as possible.

6) Passer does not set up too shallow or too deep.

7) Other receivers are sent downfield or in swing-action patterns so as to hold or decoy defensive secondary.

8) Receiver, when facing off passer waiting to receive pass, puts hands up and presents a target.

9) Screen pass is thrown not more than 15 yards.

The draw play

There is a wide variety of draw plays. Regardless of the kind, however, each and every one is designed to do the same thing. The function of the play is to "burn" the pressure type defense, by running inside the rush after encouraging pressure by action of the play. Another way of saying this is that, when the drop-back action starts, it tends to invite a defensive rush since it is natural to want to get to passer. Thus, with the opposition closing in on the quarterback, the ball is handed to a big, strong back who is difficult to stop without getting a shoulder into him.

It should go without saying that there must be drop-back action if the draw is to succeed, for it is the drop-back action that sets up this play. We do not contend that the draw cannot be run off roll-out or sprint-out action, but we do feel it is less effective from these actions.

Another aspect of the draw play is the blocking. There are two common forms of blocking on this play. The man-and-trap and cross-block are popular with a good many teams today. Almost all clubs use one or the other form of blocking. There are times though when one type of blocking is superior. For instance, using the trap technique against a defensive line that reads rather than penetrates can prove ineffective. On the other hand, man-blocking a big, strong penetrating line may prove disastrous. We therefore feel that, to really make this play effective, the draw should be blocked both ways (see Figures 8-7 and 8-8).

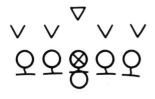

FIGURE 8–7   MAN BLOCKING

FIGURE 8–8   TRAP BLOCKING

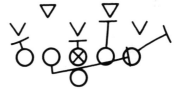

Man-blocking simply refers to each offensive lineman blocking a man, hoping to take him off his feet or force him to take an outside path. An effective rule when using man-blocking (the same as drop-back action passing rules) is that linemen should count defensive men outside the offensive center. This rule assigns the guard to block the first man and the tackle the second, while the ends block the third on their side of the center. The center blocks the man on him or to call side.

Unlike man-blocking, the trap technique does not involve the count system of blocking. Instead, a guard is asked to pull and trap the first man past the center. The other offensive linemen all block using man techniques, except the offensive man across from the man being trapped. This lineman, usually the guard, should block the first man to the outside.

Both the man-blocking technique and trap method are contingent upon several related factors. Most important is the faking of backs and the ball handling of the quarterback. And too, the ends can aid the blocking by running their patterns to look as much like an expected pass receiver as possible. Combining this united effort will lead to good, sound blocking.

SALLY RAND OR STATUE OF LIBERTY

Though not often used today, the Statue of Liberty play poses a real threat in that it features wide-openess seldom seen in the running phase of offense. Like the safety valve, screen, and draw, the Statue of Liberty depends upon the action of the drop-back pass to provide a natural opportunity for execution of the play.

How the play functions

The quarterback must drop back exactly as if he were going to pass (see Figure 8-9). If this technique is done correctly,

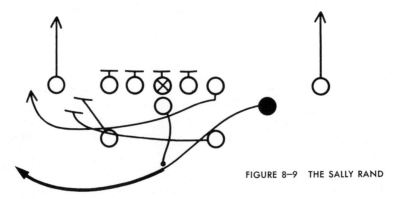

FIGURE 8–9 THE SALLY RAND

the defensive secondary should be influenced. When receivers are released in addition to the passer's action, the play becomes even more effective, since the more it looks like a pass, the better the chance for success.

After the quarterback sets up, receivers release. A back then comes behind the quarterback where the exchange is made. The ballcarrier, after being given the ball, sprints for the outside. If backs and receivers have executed well, key blocking assignments will not be difficult.

Primary blocks are on the defensive containers, namely ends and linebackers. This is so because the interior line is normally caught pursuing in a wrong direction, while the secondary finds itself so deep it has difficulty stopping the play. Defensive containers are attacked with a shoulder block, with intentions of putting them down, but at least neutralizing them until the execution of the play is carried out. A blocker is told to drive his head through the outside hip of the defender and maintain this position.

Rule blocking for Sally Rand

Interior Linemen   Each lineman should block the man in front of him. If there is no defender on his head, he then blocks the first man to the on side or in the direction the play is going. An exception to this rule is the right or offside tackle, since he will pull and lead the play.

Ends   Both ends must run a course that removes the entire defensive secondary. Generally, their route would be one that would divide the defensive halfback or wing and the safety men. By running a course midway between these defenders, whether the defense be man-to-man or zone, the secondary would tend to back-peddle.

Halfback or Tailback   The halfback or tailback's assignment is to run directly over the first man outside the block of the offensive left tackle. This will normally be the defensive end. This block should be an aggressive chop block aimed to take the defender off his feet.

Fullback   Blocking the defensive end on the on side is

the most important block of the play. This fullback block should be one of a do-or-die nature. He approaches the end at an angle that will allow his head to be between the end and ballcarrier at the point of contact.

It could be said that the Sally Rand, like other plays off drop-back action, is only as good as its execution. This is true, but it should also be said that its success depends upon being properly set up. Putting the football in the air provides for the promotion of certain excellent plays. Therefore, use of the drop-back pass becomes a *must*. Your end result will be a dynamic offense.

9

How to Put Pressure
on the Defense*

Wide-open football—this is it! The sprint-out play is not new to football, but its potential has not yet been realized by many of us coaches. The run/pass option is without doubt the best play in today's game of football. It applies more pressure on a defense than any other play because it can be either a running or passing play. The secondary of any defense defending against the option must concern itself with either playing against the run or the pass. Thus a defensive secondary is unable to stop both the running and the passing aspects of this play. Based on this premise, the option play becomes the most difficult play in football to defend against.

Our contention is that any sprint-out series should have two forms of pass patterns. They are flood pass patterns and come-back pass patterns. The flood pass pattern technique involves sending at least two, and preferably three, receivers into a predetermined zone. This zone should be an area near the position the passer will be located when the option pass play begins (see Figure 9-1).

The come-back pass pattern technique has receivers run a course similar to the flood pattern method, but at the last possible second break to a come-back position. Come-back pat-

*This chapter is based on an article entitled "The Run/Pass Option Play," by Don Read, that appeared in *Athletic Journal*, Sept., 1965.

terns can involve hooks or cut patterns (see Figures 9-2 and 9-3).

Use of motion can add effectiveness to the run/pass option play, forcing pre-play rotation of the defense. This rotation will allow an offensive team to use the throw-back pass. Utilizing the man-in-motion as a prime receiver is also a very effective technique. The man-in-motion can be used as a decoy. His motion can cause the defensive secondary to flow in the opposite direction from which the play will be going.

Depth of each pass pattern is a very important consideration. The depth a receiver will run should be decided by many factors. Position placement of defensive personnel certainly is something which affects the depth a pattern should be run. If, for example, the secondary is depth-conscious and playing nine or more yards deep, shorter cuts may be most efficient. On the other hand, if a team is playing its halfbacks seven or less yards off the line of scrimmage, perhaps deeper patterns would be more valid.

Another element that must be considered when judging depth of a pattern is a team's field position. For example, running a flood pattern to the short side is difficult unless patterns are run deeper than normal. When near the goal line, patterns are automatically reduced in depth because of the lack of field in which to run.

A third factor in determining depth of a pattern is the scouting report on your opponent. A defensive halfback's speed, agility, and overall potential can be determined through scouting. This type of information enables a team to choose the best pass patterns and the most advantageous course to run against opposition.

The sprint-out play can add or generate a great deal of punch in any team's offense, because it is the only play in football which contains both the threat of the running play and the danger of the pass.

BACKFIELD TECHNIQUES

Backfield responsibilities should be kept very simple, each back having a basic assignment. Assuming the formation is an

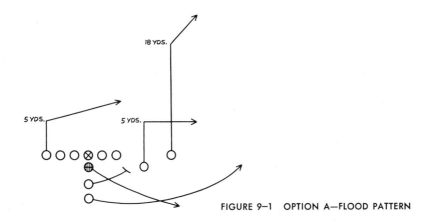

FIGURE 9–1   OPTION A—FLOOD PATTERN

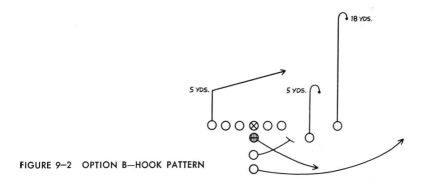

FIGURE 9–2   OPTION B—HOOK PATTERN

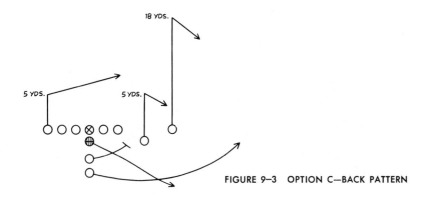

FIGURE 9–3   OPTION C—BACK PATTERN

"I" set, the fullback blocks the first man outside his own offensive tackle, to the call side. Most of the time this is a defensive end. The fullback is taught to block his man with a shoulder block and try to knock him off his feet. His head must be in front of the body of the defensive man—between the ball-carrier and the enemy.

The tailback is sent on a swing pattern, placed in motion, or used as a lead blocker, depending on the call. This back is used as a safety valve when in swing action. If pressure is placed on the passer, the tailback will receive the ball quickly from the quarterback.

The remaining halfback is expected to be a prime receiver in the play and will run the pattern called. This remaining back can line up in a variety of positions and still be a prime receiver. Occasionally he can be sent in motion in the opposite direction of the play to create a decoy and perhaps force some form of rotation away from the play.

The quarterback, as the exchange is made with the center, should step back from the center with his foot to the side that the play is directed, at about a 45-degree angle. After the exchange and step-back, the ball should be brought up to chest height. Laces should be adjusted for grip and passing as the second and third steps are made. A depth of about five to seven yards should be established as soon as possible. When correct depth is apparent, the quarterback reads the defensive end or outside man. If this man is coming tough, the passer must toss the ball to the swing man (tailback) immediately. The ball should be carried high so as to establish a passing threat. Pumping the ball as if to pass can be effective and help hold the defensive secondary. It is a must that the quarterback begin upfield before throwing the ball. There is no option if this is not done. It is the moving upfield and pumping the ball that challenges a secondary.

If the play turns out to be a pass, it is absolutely necessary to be facing in the direction of the receiver. The body should follow through as the ball is released. Passing on the run requires tossing the ball much softer than normal and with plenty of lead.

Throwing the ball on the run is somewhat different than throwing from a standing position. There must be a much greater emphasis on specific techniques; namely, the position of arms and feet. It is important that arms be carried high while sprinting out and that the arm cock no deeper than the ear of the passer. The ball should be thrown a little closer to the body than from the set position to insure power and stability. As the football comes forward in the throwing process, the elbow of the passing arm should precede the rest of the arm, insuring the whipping action needed to get the ball to its destination rapidly.

Another factor that deserves stress is the necessity of throwing off the front leg rather than the rear, in the drop-back method of passing action. A sprint-out passer throws on the run with his body moving forward, and is forced to throw off the momentum of his body. Contrary to the drop-back passer who is moving back to set up on his back leg, the sprint-out passer must plant his front foot to deliver the ball. For a right-handed passer, this would mean the right foot; for a left hander, the left foot. The lead foot should point in the direction the pass will travel. The trailing leg will act as the following-through phase of the maneuver.

A sprint-out should be delivered as close to the line of scrimmage as possible. The play is designed as a running play first and a passing play second. Passers are instructed to run anytime they can to get a first down, regardless of the score or time remaining. This is advocated because, with receivers downfield, the defensive secondary responsibility is normally to play the receivers first and the run second. Thus, if the quarterback reaches the point of decision (to run or pass), it is probable that several yards can be obtained by running the ball.

LINEMAN TECHNIQUES

Because the sprint-out pass is a major part of any sound passing attack, a good portion of offensive practice time must be allowed for perfection of the play. Linemen have an extremely prominent role in this play, so the techniques used to make the play go must be highly refined. It is therefore suggested that approximately twenty minutes each day be allowed for execution of this play. Linemen are taught basic maneuvers and work daily on each.

Before the techniques can be explored, however, it should be said that having one rule of blocking which applies to all interior linemen is desirable: *They block the first man to the on side or side the play is going. If there is not a defensive man to call the side, pull and lead.* As stated in the rule, linemen are asked to "reach or over-block" to the call side, or pull and lead the play. Some coaches feel that over-blocking is very difficult. It is agreed this method takes time to develop, but it can be a very effective form of blocking.

This block has been used for years with great success. The most common, consistent, and effective method of reach-blocking is attained by using a reverse shoulder block. Teaching this skill starts by making a short step with the near foot straight down the line of scrimmage, while at the same time throwing the near shoulder back as if pulling. The far shoulder is directed at the mid-section of the opponent. Like a near shoulder block, it is hoped that the blocker will not go to the ground. We preach that it is better to over-lead the opposition than under-lead. Blocking behind the defender will not cut him off, thus allowing defensive penetration into the backfield. If, on the other hand, the blocker over-leads on the block, a cross-body block can still be applied, effectively preventing penetration.

Tight end

The tight end's assignment on this differs slightly from that of the other linemen. His responsibility on the sprint-out play to the right is first, to reach-block to right and cut off anyone to his inside. If it is felt this block is not necessary, the tight end can run a trail pattern to act as a secondary receiver. The end himself is the best judge of his own assignment.

Pulling interior linemen

We see no reason for not pulling any of the interior linemen. If they have no one to block, they are wasted if they remain on the line of scrimmage. We ask pulling linemen to step
back at about a 45-degree angle on the first step. This will vary
a little from position to position. The farther the position
from the center, the flatter the pull. For example, a tackle's
pull would be much shallower than a guard or center. As the
first step is made, the arm to the side of the play should also
be thrown back by a pull or jerk with the arm and elbow.
The back foot follows the lead foot out, keeping about ten to
twelve inches between feet. The body should, at this point, be
in a football position (ready to tackle, block, or run). The
next consideration is to maintain this semi-crouch position
two to three steps. Arms should be kept high like a sprinter,
and weight forward on the balls of the feet.

The assignment for a pulling lineman is to block the outside man on the line of scrimmage. If two linemen have pulled
on the play, both men will put the defensive man down. Often
it will be found that the fullback is blocking the same man. In
any sprint-out play, the most important defensive man to
eliminate is the outside—the end, cornerbacker, or wing, depending on the defense.

To destroy the outside man, a shoulder block should be
used. If the shoulder block is not sustained, the blocker should
roll into either a reverse-body or cross-body block. The important thing is getting this defensive containment down. If
the defensive man over-penetrates, the function of pulling
linemen is to kick him out. This will lead to running the sprint-
out inside the defensive containment.

SPRINT-OUT PLAY TO THE LEFT

The effectiveness of the sprint-out play is increased if it is
run to the offensive left side as well as the right side. The

sprint-out play to the left, for a right-handed passer, offers
more problems than does the same play to the right. When a
right-hander runs to his left, the pass is strictly an arm pass,
since his body is moving away from the direction of his throwing arm.

Because it is important to be able to sprint out both to the
right and to the left, special consideration must be made to
compensate for the problem. Throwing the ball while running to the left is something like a second baseman's double-
play relay. The ball is thrown against or across the body
with the right arm while moving to the left. Two techniques
to overcome this disadvantage are the side-arm pass and extra-
depth method.

Side-arm passing

This is easy to do since it is almost a natural thing when
a right hander runs to the left. Play execution is exactly like
sprint-out to the right.

Extra depth

To adopt this method, the passer must sprint out deeper
than the normal five to eight yards. It is recommended that a
quarterback get about eight to ten yards deep when going to
the left. This depth insures the passer enough room to be
moving upfield when the ball is thrown. This technique allows
the passer to throw the ball in the same manner as he does
when moving to the right. Acquiring additional depth allows
the shoulders and body to gain their proper relationship with
the runner. We call this "squaring up."

Over the years we have found the second method most receptive and protective. Teaching play this way, though, requires constant attention. Most passers seem to revert back to
running a flat course while sprinting out to the left. Coaching
emphasis on facing downfield when releasing the ball will help
instill this concept.

CONCLUSION

Whether it be a sprint-out play to the right or to the left, the fact remains that this play places a defense in the most disadvantageous position possible. It is the greatest play in football—the sprint-out—the play that wins games for you!

10

How to Keep the
Defense Honest

Dangerous, but necessary is perhaps the best description for the throw-back pass. Yes, it is a gamble, but effective it can be, if given the right time and situation. We believe if you are to utilize the sprint-out play, the throw-back pass has to be used. This is because the best counter-play off sprint-out action is the throw-back.

The main function of the throw-back pass is to prevent the defensive secondary from over-rotating when pursuing the flow of the play. The best way to stop the sprint-out play is to contain and pressure it. This can be done by a rotation of the secondary to the side the sprint-out is being executed. When a team reads the sprint-out and pressures it with wings, cornerbacks, halfbacks, or safeties, the running aspect of the play is taken away and an offense is forced to throw.

Since a defense is allowed to pursue or rotate immediately with the flow of the play, pass patterns can often be cut off. The sprint-out pass can be taken away from a team if the off-side safety on an umbrella defense, or the off-side halfback on a three-deep secondary is permitted to cover the on-side deep passing zone. Then if a defense forces with the on-side halfback and covers with an off-side defense, the offense must counter this action or disregard the sprint-out play.

The throw-back pass, if off sprint-out action, should look as much like the sprint-out play as possible. Blocking rules can be practically identical to the sprint-out play. An exception is the peel-back of a halfback to the side away from the sprint-out action.

Patterns that can be run off this action are numerous, more commonly used patterns being flares and hooks. Passes can be thrown to either the end or the halfback away from the action of the play (see Figures 10-1 and 10-2).

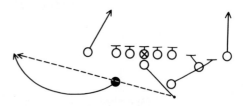

FIGURE 10–1   3-COUNT SYSTEM—90 SWING LOOK-IN THROW-BACK

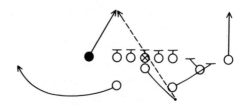

FIGURE 10–2   3-COUNT SYSTEM—90 LOOK-IN SWING THROW-BACK

HOW A PASS SHOULD BE THROWN

A real key to the success of the throw-back play is the work of the quarterback. If he really makes the play look like the sprint-out, chances increase of making the play go. It is the *action* that starts the flow of the secondary. The quarterback should set up directly behind his offensive tackle. Depth of the set-up should be about that of the drop-back action. As the passer starts to set up, he should plant his right foot (assuming he is right-handed), bending his leg slightly at the knee. The ball should come up to the throwing position as the passer plants his feet. The front leg will point in the direction of the receiver as the ball is released.

It must be remembered that the throw-back pass is not one used often. We compare the throw-back off sprint-out action play to the reverse play that acts as a counter for the running game. The throw-back pass used wisely is a fine play. It is certainly a play difficult to defend against. In addition, the threat of this play keeps a defense honest, resulting in a defense that stays at home rather than over-pursues.

WHEN THE DEFENSE READS THE PLAY

With the increased distance the ball must travel on this play, adding to the probability of interceptions, a passer must be overly cautious with the throw. Instructing the quarterback to dump the ball in the bleachers, if a defender is blanketing a receiver, is good advice. A drill involving the passer's evaluating the placement of defensive men while executing the play, is helpful. This drill helps the quarterback determine when to pass and when to toss the ball away. We tell our passers it's better to get rid of the ball four times than have one intercepted! Again, the concept is—read the secondary, then deliver the pigskin either to the receiver or no one!

SETTING UP THE PLAY

Unlike the sprint-out, the throw-back must be used sparingly. It is therefore very important that it be set up properly. Calling the play too early in a contest, or before the sprint-out play has been run several times, is not sound. A satisfactory philosophy regarding this play is never to use it in the first quarter, and not more than once each remaining quarter. We stick to this rule and, in addition, do not allow our quarterbacks to call the play. When the appropriate time arrives to run the throw-back, the play is sent in from the bench.

USE OF FIELD POSITION

Field position is of importance to the function of all plays, but particularly so on the throw-back play. Room for the play to operate is a determining factor in its success or failure. There must be adequate space laterally, as well as plenty of yards from the opposition's goal line. Based on this criteria, the ideal field position to have when the play is called is between the 30-yard lines and at a hashmark. From this location the play can be run to the wide side of the field and deep enough to beat the secondary rotation or coverage.

SELECTING APPROPRIATE SETS

The formation from which the throw-back pass is run is not significant, but with one exception—it must reflect or relate to the set used to run the sprint-out play. If, for example, the sprint-out play is run from a pro set, it is advisable to do the same with the throw-back. Thus the clue for detecting a tendency is eliminated.

It is suggested, however, that being able to use a play from more than one set and from several patterns is advantageous. Again the important concern is to be able to run the sprint-out from the same basic formation.

TYPES OF PATTERNS

Some of the various routes that can be used, and descriptive terminology of each, are shown in Chapter 7. The more highly regarded throw-back patterns are diagramed in this chapter in Figures 10-1, 10-2, 10-3 and 10-4. By utilizing names or descriptive terms, a variety of patterns can be employed. Greater flexibility is provided. In reference to Chapter 7, it should be emphasized here that, adopting names rather than numbers results in simplicity.

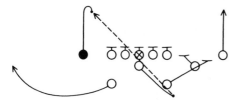

FIGURE 10–3   3-COUNT SYSTEM—90 HOOK SWING THROW-BACK

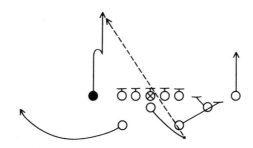

FIGURE 10–4   4-COUNT SYSTEM—90 HOOK-GO SWING THROW-BACK

If, for example, the throw-back play is called using the swing pattern as the call, the terms "swing deep," "swing out," "swing in," and "swing back" can supply great variety to the play. The beauty of this form of pattern calling is that nine footballers carry out their single assignments regardless of the direction of the swing call, while only two people must be concerned with the pass directly. Figures 10-1 to 10-4 point out how the use of terms or names helps simplify the play.

To provide additional simplicity, the order of descriptive terms suggests primary and secondary receivers. For instance a call such as "90 Hook-swing" directs the tight end to hook and receive the pass. The near back to the tight end side runs the swing pattern; if the play was "90 Swing-hook," prime receiver would be the near back; secondary receiver, the tight end, runs the hook.

After patterns have been stated in order, there remains the action of the play to be called. Again by using descriptive terms this facet becomes equally elementary. A throw-back pass then could be called "90 Swing-hook throw-back." This completes the cycle of the call, with the exception of putting a man-in-motion into the pattern or utilized as a decoy. To accomplish this, the name of the back is called after all other aspects of the play. When the backs name is called, he then proceeds in motion to the call side unless the term "away" is used. To place a man-in-motion in the pattern, the play might be "90 Swing-hook throw-back Rip." The play would be as mentioned above, but Rip would go in motion to the 90 or call side. A "Rip away" call would tell Rip to go in motion to 80 or away from the call side.

THE COUNT SYSTEM

When using the throw-back pass, it is particularly helpful to adapt the count method of passing, which involves the time aspect of the pass delivery. Passer and receiver both count simultaneously, from the time the ball is snapped to the time the ball is released. This provides both parties the advantage of knowing exactly when the ball is to be thrown. The count system should be used in two ways: when throwing the short quick pass, and when throwing the middle range or intermediate pass. With the shorter pass such as a look-in, hook, or swing, the three-count system is used. Patterns that fall into the ten- to twenty-yard range are considered intermediate passes and adapt well to the four-count system.

This type of timing is ideal for the throw-back play, since both passer and receiver can make the play look more like the sprint-out. There is no need to be turning and looking for the receiver or passer until the time is right.

When using the three-count system, passers are taught to set on the right leg (if right-handed), in a right-left-right step procedure. This should place the passer about four yards deep and between the tackle and guard. As the steps are being completed, the ball must come up to the throwing position. When the right foot sets up, the ball must be ready to be released.

If the four-count technique is selected, the quarterback

will set up using the right-left-right-left-right manner. The angle of the set-up should be *much* deeper on the four-count method, keeping the throwing position from both the three- and four-count techniques between the guard and tackle. The difference is primarily in sprinting back. The four-count pro- cedure sets up at about seven yards deep.

A count system provides perfection and timing. The danger of an unsuccessful play is somewhat diminished, making it rea- sonably safe for use. And it should be remembered that when the throw-back pass goes, it goes big!

ANYTHING WORTHWHILE IS A GAMBLE

Dramatic—hazardous—at times frustrating—this is the throw- back pass. But it's hard to detect and difficult to defend against. And it keeps the defense honest!

11

How to Develop
an Explosive
Passing Attack

The most explosive play in the game of football today is the play-action pass. Generally it is unlike the drop-back pass and the sprint-out pass, but it is similar to the drop-back in that it allows the pass to be set up rather than thrown on the run. The play-action pass is like the sprint-out pass in that it develops off a running-action play. We might say then that the play-action combines some features of both the drop-back and sprint-out plays.

DEFENSIVE VULNERABILITY

The play-action pass can be the most effective of all forms of passes in that it is difficult to defend against. A defensive secondary's first reaction, particularly linebackers, is to read and diagnose the running action of the play. Therefore, it tends to hold or freeze the secondary while a pass pattern is being run.

Since play-action passes are so difficult to defend against, this aspect of passing should be well developed in an offense.

Producing the play-action pass requires good timing and execution. The play must look like a running play even though it is a pass.

A most effective way of adapting this method of passing to an offense is by patterning passing plays off your most successful running plays. If the off-tackle power is the best running play in your offense, it is wise to throw a pass off this action.

COMPLEMENTARY PLAYS

Certain running plays tend to complement the play-action pass better than others. The dive or slant-action running plays usually are good for this purpose. So a pass play that resembles this movement probably will function well, providing running plays are used in conjunction with passing plays. It is not feasible to acquire play-action passes without using running plays to set up the pass.

Pass patterns that can effectively be adopted to play-action passes are limited to some degree by their nature. These routes have to begin as if the play is a run. A typical pattern that might be injected is one that starts with the receiver faking a block on a defensive man and then running his course. Some often-used play-action patterns are square-out, zone, V-out, and streak. Of course, the pattern used should be determined by needed yardage, field position, and abilities of personnel.

QUARTERBACK IS THE KEY

A quarterback can make or break this play. He has two important responsibilities—*faking* and *passing*. Faking on every play is important to a play's execution and outcome, but play-action passes are completely dependent upon the ball-handling aspect of the play. The play-action pass also demands perfect timing on delivery of the ball.

Faking

When teaching ball handling, instruct the quarterback to keep the ball close to his body at belt buckle height. He should keep his shoulders rounded, head tilted downward, and knees and waist bent as much as possible. It is important for the quarterback to keep his back to the line of scrimmage throughout the entire action of the play. Hands and arms should cover the ball to eliminate it from view. This is an ideal hand-off position and one that provides for excellent faking.

We believe all hand-offs should be made with one hand unless it is a belly-type play. By using a one-hand exchange, the ball can be hidden longer and more effectively, encouraging the defense to defend against a run while the offense prepares to pass. The longer the play looks like a run the greater the chance for completing a pass. Good faking will bring about success.

Of the entire ball-handling process, following through with good head and eye action is the most important aspect. As long as possible, the quarterback must watch the action of the back after the initial fake has been made. This means hiding the ball against the stomach while the head and eyes look in the direction of the faking back.

Passing

Timing the sequence of the play, as well as the setting up and delivery of the pass, is crucial. If the ball is thrown too soon, the receiver will not have made his final break or looked toward the passer in time. Equally as disastrous is the pass being tossed too late. This is the number one cause of interceptions. Therefore, perfection of a play-action pass takes sound execution of running and faking of the play, as well as timing and delivery of the football.

On the following pages are diagramed some play-action pass plays. Each of these is sound in its own right. The exact selection should be based upon the running offense used. It is worth

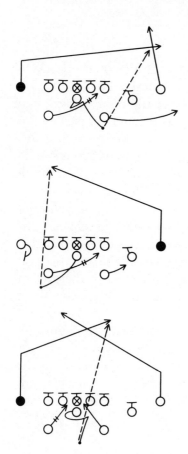

FIGURE 11–1 PLAY-ACTION PASSES

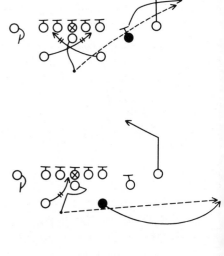

FIGURE 11–2 PLAY-ACTION PASSES

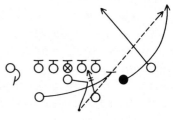

noting that all plays shown in Figures 11-1 and 11-2 are of the deeper-pattern nature.

AGGRESSIVE BLOCKING

Similar to a running play, the play-action pass allows the line to fire out with an aggressive block. This form of blocking not only provides for running-type blocking, but it supplies the defense with what looks like a running play.

The most effective way of accomplishing an aggressive block is with the butt block. Though many coaches frown on this block, it nonetheless is a very good technique. Blockers are taught to block in the same manner as they do on the running play, on which the play-action pass is patterned. The progressive phases of the block are:

1) Release from stance with head up and forearms coming up to chest height.
2) Legs kept under body at about shoulder width. It is important that body is not over-extended so that there is enough explosion to follow through.
3) Head must ward off charge of opponent as it is placed at the bottom of opponent's numbers.
4) Position must be maintained to prevent enemy from sliding to the offensive side where ball is being thrown.
5) Legs keep churning as arms and head lift man being blocked.

There are two important coaching points that will aid in establishing the butt block technique. Ignored, either or both of these points can cause an unsuccessful block. More often than not, when this block is not made properly, the fault is due to poor arm position or keeping the eyes closed. Poor arm position refers to not getting the arms up to supply a larger blocking surface on which to catch the opposition if he slips off the helmet and shoulders. Keeping the eyes closed will lead to missed blocks and improper position.

WHEN AND WHERE TO USE THE PLAY-ACTION PASS

Down and distance obviously have something to do with play selection. The play-action pass, however, is one of the few plays in football that can be executed without defensive anticipation on any down regardless of yardage. Like all plays, though, it is especially appropriate at given times. Great success generally will prevail if the situation seems geared to a run. Second or third down and short yardage is an ideal time to use the play-action pass. Still another situation that may warrant this play is on or near your opponent's goal line. It is particularly good here because defenses generally increase the number of personnel on the line of scrimmage, while decreasing the number of secondarymen. This in turn makes them more vulnerable to the forward pass.

The play-action pass should never be used prior to running the play to which it is related. As stated earlier, it is recommended that the related play be called several times before using the play-action pass. With sequences used as suggested, it becomes extremely difficult for a defense to guard against the play regardless of field position or down and distance to go.

Usually, the play-action pass is a long-type pass, since the action takes time to develop. Good faking by backs and your quarterback will help promote success of the play. When proper timing and good receiving is added, the play becomes unstoppable.

WHY NOT BE EXPLOSIVE?

Analyze, criticize, improvise—but *use* the play-action pass! Ask yourself, "Why not be explosive?"

12

Coaching to Prevent
Interceptions

Let me assure you that a forward pass can be as
safe as a run—you can make it what you want. In short, the
threat of an interception can only be eliminated if the coach
himself believes it can be done and takes specific steps to see
that it becomes a reality.

ELIMINATING THE INTERCEPTION

The chance of an interception being made by the defense
is in direct relation to two factors: (1) the physical and mental
capability of the defense; and (2) an offense's ability to execute the best type of pass play at the most precise time. Since
there is little an offense can do to control the first factor, it is
important to explore well the latter consideration. The question now might be asked, "What is the best pass play?" How
does one determine which play is the safest? It is our contention that several elements contribute to preventing interceptions, and thus there is no simple answer. These precautionary
measures are the theme of this chapter.

USE INDIVIDUAL PATTERNS

We feel that generally the fewer receivers that are directed into a passing play, the better the play's chances for success. The reason for this is that individual patterns provide for the split-second timing so necessary for completions. The passer need not concern himself with the routes of several receivers —which helps him concentrate on one man and, most of the time, on one defender. Common sense will tell you that a person can be more accurate if he restricts his attention to one man. The human eye is much like a telescope—the wider it is opened, the broader the scope of the picture. The more concentrated the focus, the more detail seen. We believe if a quarterback can concentrate his efforts on one man he will be better able to get the ball to the receiver at the most appropriate time.

A second significant reason for using individual patterns is that it affords maximum protection for the passer. Without question, the defensive pass rush causes more interceptions than any other factor. Using pass plays with individual routes provides a quarterback with extra blockers, thus allowing more time to throw. Obviously, the less pressure a passer has to contend with, the greater his chances of perfecting delivery.

STATIONARY TECHNIQUE

Years of observation have led us to believe that a much larger percentage of passes can be completed if either the receiver or passer is stationary while executing a play. In other words, if the passer sets up (such as he would in drop-back play), half-rolls, or pulls up on the sprint, he can be firmly planted when releasing the football, and he will be more accurate. If the passer is not set, we believe it is important that the receiver be stationary. Patterns like hooks and curls provide this feature and are tough to stop.

The advantages of keeping a passer or receiver stationary are that a passer has a better balance and follow-through, and the tendency for mechanical error (such as the nose of the ball being down) is lessened. A receiver being stationary is in the best position for viewing the play and has a better chance for catching the football.

The above philosophy can be tested by hanging a tire from your goal post and having your passers record how many balls they throw through the tire from a stationary stance compared to throws from a running position. You can also chart your receivers making stationary receptions versus moving catches during your passing drills. We think you will be convinced of and surprised at the results.

THROW THE BALL LOW

The toughest pass to intercept is the one thrown low. There are, of course, many patterns where it is necessary to get the ball up in the air, but much of the time it is most important to keep the football as close to the ground as possible. A ball thrown up in the air many times is up for grabs more often. It affords the chance of being batted around, hitting part of a body and bouncing off, and allows the defender a better opportunity of getting his hands on the ball. A pass thrown low forces the receiver to protect the football from defenders since he must reach down and bring his body around the ball.

PUT SOMETHING ON THE BALL

We firmly believe that if a pass is thrown with some zip on it, the chances of interception are lessened. Interceptions occur when a defensive man has time to react and get to the ball. The longer the football is in the air, the greater the chance of interception. Good passers throw the football hard. The best passers, in this modern age of football, without exception have strong arms. The old theory of throwing the ball softly has little merit in today's game of football. We feel, on most pass plays, the quarterback can try to throw the ball right through the receiver. The exception, of course, is the deep pass that must have height.

GET POSITION ON DEFENSIVE MAN

A receiver can do a lot to prevent interceptions by aligning himself correctly with the passer. A cardinal sin is for a receiver to let a defender have a straight line to the ball once it has been thrown. Receivers should always be able to cut a defender off or out-position him to the ball, unless the ball is thrown behind him. There is *no excuse* for being *out-desired* for the football! This principle alone will eliminate many interceptions.

We think that if a defender intercepts a pass that is on target, we should be able to defeat this man regularly with completions. In short, if an opposing player is playing our receiver that close, we should be able to beat him deep or with a cutting pattern. We emphasize again, *no defensive secondary-man should be allowed to have an equally good position on the ball, regardless of the ability or speed of the offensive man.*

USE THE SHORT PASS

The shorter the pass, the greater the chance of completion! This seems obvious, yet so often the passing attacks of many teams are geared around the longer pass. How many times have you seen a team behind by a touchdown or two trying to play "catch up" with the bomb? A sound passing attack is one that can, like the good running team, have ball control. The percentage of short passes thrown in a given game should far outnumber the deeper ones. Statistics from my high school coaching career indicate that we completed but one of seven passes thrown over twenty yards. These same stats show that one in every fourteen passes thrown over twenty yards was intercepted. From these facts we conclude that the longer the pass is thrown, the greater the opportunity for interception.

OUT PATTERNS ARE BEST

Contrary to what many football scholars believe, there is much less chance of a pass being intercepted if it is thrown to an isolated receiver running an out, hook, hitch, or sideline pattern. We do not contend that this type of play offers complete safety from interception. Like any play, if the ball is thrown poorly or the receiver runs a sloppy pattern, there is always the chance of the opposition grabbing off the football. It is our belief, however, that an out pattern limits the number of defenders, thus cutting down on the possibility of interceptions. Regardless of the type of secondary coverage used, the middle area of a secondary always has more people, because coverage comes not only from the middle, but from both sides. Therefore, short pass routes over the middle tend to be vulnerable to interceptions.

WORK ON DETACHED RECEIVERS

The most difficult men for defenders to cover are detached or spread receivers. Because an isolated receiver has a lot of running room, he is more difficult to cover. It is almost impossible to take both the inside and outside patterns away with a single defender. Thus, many teams are forced to cover the detached receiver with more than one man. We suggest that if a team does not respect spread receivers by covering them with more than one defender, an offense should repeatedly throw to these receivers. If a detached receiver and passer have any ability, and work on this combination, they will be hard to stop.

MOTION CAN HELP

One of the real offensive values of motion is the physical and mental distraction it creates for a defensive secondary. We contend that when a man is running within a defender's line of vision, it causes an over-awareness on the part of this player, whether he is responsible for this man or not. This defensive man's capability is lessened because he has been distracted—this is especially true with respect to linebackers and secondarymen.

Another feature of motion is that, in some instances, it may cause a pre-rotation or force defenders to change their responsibility. For example, when playing against a monster-type defense, motion away from the monster might encourage the monster, if he is declared to that side, to rotate with the flow. This could enable an end or back to the side away from motion to be isolated with one defender (see Figure 12-1).

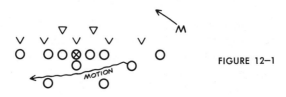

FIGURE 12-1

An offense employing a wing "T" offense that places its wingback in motion could (against a man-to-man defense) force the defensive secondary to defend against a different receiver than originally assigned, or perhaps change their coverage to zone. Again the advantage here is that it adds confusion and is a distraction to a defense (see Figures 12-2 and 12-3.

ESTABLISH SOUND PASS PROTECTION

Pass protection is a very important aspect of preventing interceptions because the best pass defense is a good pass rush. The type of protection is not necessarily the answer to sound protection. Man-to-man, zone or combination protection all are satisfactory. *What is important* is that every defensive man on

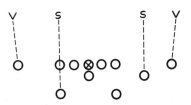

FIGURE 12–2   RESPONSIBILITY WITHOUT MOTION

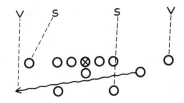

FIGURE 12–3   POSSIBLE RESPONSIBILITY CHANGES WITH MOTION

the line of scrimmage and those that pose a rushing threat (namely linebackers) are blocked by someone. Since it is sometimes difficult to accomplish this, a lot of time must be devoted to this phase of football. Drills, both live and dummy, should be utilized regularly if sound protection is to be developed. Emphasis on pass protection in practice will reap great dividends.

THE PASSER MUST COVER

Although a passer's covering or acting as a safety, once the ball has been thrown, does not reduce interceptions, it nonetheless can prevent a score. There is only one way a passer will effectively and continually carry out this deed. He must drill on it regularly. Like any other phase of football, covering must become an instinct. It is not a natural thing, and this needs to be emphasized to passers. We consider covering a second effort, and tell our passers that without second effort we will not win a game. The rule our passers use when covering is to release to the side the ball is thrown as soon as the pass is in the air, its purpose being to take a path that will intercept the enemy in case the ball is intercepted.

USE BEST RECEIVER

One of the biggest mistakes in our opinion made by many of us coaches is not utilizing the talent we have. Every team has its "best" receiver. It is just good logic to capitalize on this footballer's talent. Percentages are with you if the ball is thrown to this receiver as often as a team can get away with it. Certainly the pattern an individual runs is of major importance; equally so is having the best man running the pattern. There are few successful teams in the game today that do not have *one* leading or outstanding receiver.

WORK ON WEAKNESS OF DEFENSE

Every secondary alignment has its strength and weakness. Taking advantage of the various alignments can greatly reduce the chance of interception; although this is discussed in the following chapter, some examples here may be appropriate. A slant-in type pattern is hard to complete against a defense that has cornerbackers or walk-away ends. Using hook or curl patterns is far more difficult against a man-for-man defense, as compared to a zone coverage. Throw-back passes are much more successful against a rotating defense. Combination patterns are particularly good against a zone secondary.

SOME MORE PHILOSOPHY

In today's well-coached style of football, teams prepare thoroughly for a particular game. They possess much knowledge of the opposition's potential, philosophy of play, and offensive tendencies. Having this thorough understanding of the enemy, a defensive team can be amazingly successful in predicting run or pass. For this reason a team should avoid passing tendencies. Throwing the ball primarily when behind, or only on third down, is not sound football. These are situations when passing successfully is the most difficult, because the defense expects the ball to be in the air.

Teams that have good luck moving the ball, generally pass on any down and from any place on the field. This kind of football puts the defense at a disadvantage, since they are less able to predict pass or run. This not only helps the passing game, but makes the running offense more effective. From the standpoint of passing, if this thinking is adhered to, there will be more completed passes and less interceptions.

13

Scouting the Opponent's Pass Defense

Confidence in you, your coaches, and your total football program is readily instilled in players through good, efficient scouting reports. There is great comfort in knowing the opponent's ability. This secure feeling will carry over into a game, helping calm players' nerves and resulting in good, heads-up football from kickoff to final gun.

In a game featuring two evenly matched teams, the club that has been most completely informed will win. An informed team will make fewer mistakes, be able to execute the big play, and take advantage of the enemy's weaknesses. A well-schooled team is like a highly disciplined army—*hard to beat!*

The type of pass offense a team will pit against another should depend largely upon scouting reports of an opponent's pass defense. Decisions to emphasize play-action passes, the sprint-out or drop-back, must be based on knowledge acquired through scouting. Types of patterns and specific ways to put the football in the air are relative to these reports. Obviously, then, scouting a secondary's ability to defend against the forward pass is most important. The more information compiled on the secondary, the better the chance an aerial team will have of exploiting them.

There is no formula or pat procedure for scouting. Scouting

should be geared to what your particular needs are. The forms or techniques presented here do not furnish all the answers; rather, they reflect what has worked best for our program and has met our needs. We do hope, however, that these methods will provide you with some ideas and information that will help you accomplish an effective job of scouting the defensive secondary.

RECOGNIZING THE SECONDARY

Defensive secondaries have adopted a variety of alignments in recent years—which tends to complicate offensive football. A team advocating the passing game has been forced to recognize these position placements and adapt accordingly. The magnitude of changes created, not only in the placement of secondary people, but also in the number of specialists, has dictated the kind of aerial attack chosen.

An offense today must have the ability to attack any defense with a wide range of passing plays. Being able to *read* an opponent's alignment can be a tremendous help in determining which pattern to run and how to run it. For example,

FIGURE 13–1　DEFENSIVE SECONDARY SETS

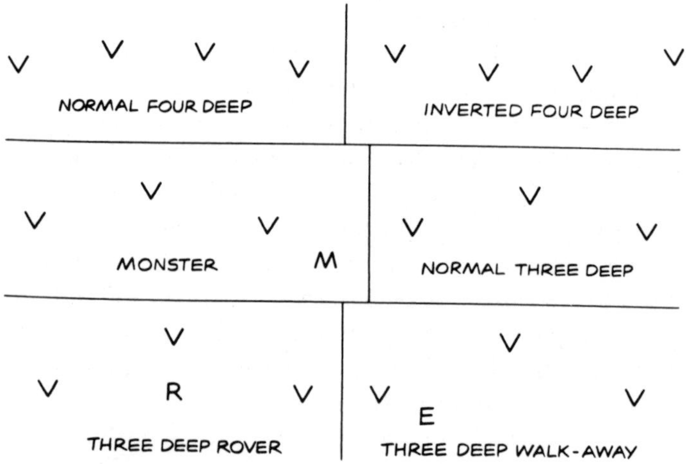

the probability of completing a look-in pass to the split end
when the defense has placed a man in a walk-away position
is unlikely. It is equally difficult to flood a zone against a four-
deep secondary. On the other hand, the sprint-out play normally succeeds well in a three-deep system (see Figure 13-1).

Position placement of the secondary also affects the timing
of the throw. Where the defense lines up has a bearing on releasing the ball early or late. If executing a square-in pattern
(see Chapter 7) against an inverted four-deep defense, the
ball should be thrown late, allowing it to be caught between
the two safeties. One last example of timing the throw according to where the defense is stationed, is passing immediately
after the cut is made, on a sideline-type course, when playing
against a three-deep club.

ADJUSTMENTS AND POSITION CHART

A big help in exacting the position adjustment of a defensive secondary is an Adjustment and Position Chart (Figure
13-2). This form allows space to draw in the defensive halfbacks and safeties after they have adjusted to a flanker or split
end. Position of these secondarymen can be shown in relation to the offensive receiver in terms of depth and alignment.

FIGURE 13–2

ADJUSTMENTS AND

POSITION CHART

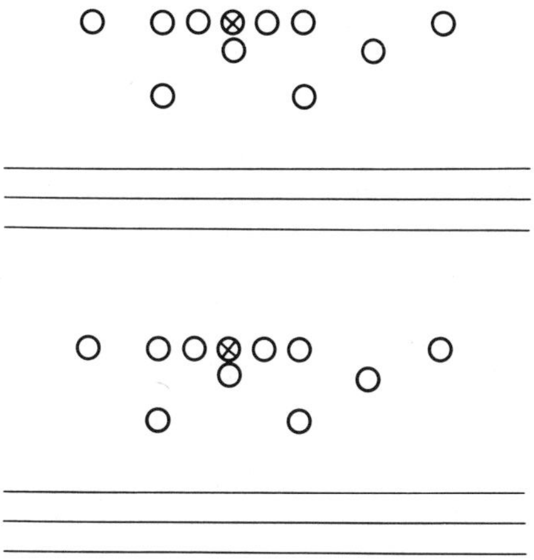

The number of yards the detached man splits, and his distance from the receiver, should be placed on the form.

This chart is particularly valuable to receivers in preparing for a game. Specific moves and patterns are naturally better against defenders who are shown taking an improper position on receivers. Quarterbacks can also profit from this form in that it points out what plays might best succeed against a given secondary.

DETERMINING THE COVERAGE

Closely allied with position placement is determining the kind of coverage a team is using. The three basic forms of coverage are zone, man-to-man, and combination. Knowing the method of coverage the opposition uses limits or encourages specific patterns and plays. As a rule, patterns that are most satisfactory against a man-to-man form of coverage are deep and crossing patterns. Against a zone approach, flood and individual patterns prove to be the most effective. Look-ins, hooks, swings, and curl patterns are hard to stop with a zone defense. This is because players' attitudes are centered around responsibility for an area, rather than for a man.

SCOUTING THE SECONDARY

When scouting the opposition, it is important to rate the defensive personnel according to their ability to defend against the forward pass. Suggested principles which can act as guidelines for evaluation purposes are:

1) Can any of the defensive people be beaten deep?
2) Does any of the backs turn his back to the ball?
3) What is emotional reaction of back when a pass is completed in his area?
4) Is there any defender that lines up with improper body position?

5) What is depth of secondary? Is there any secondaryman that tends to stay too deep or plays a man too loose?

6) Do any of the backs have a tendency to get legs crossed when defending?

7) What are sizes of those in secondary?

8) What is basic adjustment to split ends, flankers, slots, wings, and heavy sets?

9) When motion is used what type of coverage, such as rotation, develops?

10) What is defensive adjustment to sprint-out or roll-out passes?

11) Do linebackers react into passing zones if drop-back action is shown?

12) What is pass responsibility of ends?

If each of the above mentioned questions can be answered, a very efficient scouting report of an opponent's secondary can be constructed. This knowledge can serve as the basis for preparing your pass offense for this team. There is, though, one other form of evaluation that can act as a supplement to scouting the secondary—rating the speed and reaction of defensive backs.

RATING SPEED AND REACTION

The most difficult aspect of scouting is measuring speed and reaction ability of a future opponent. Because it is so intangible, many scouts neglect this phase of scouting. If done accurately, however, knowing the opposition's overall speed and ability to react can be of great aid. This is especially valuable to your receivers, who will be running patterns against these players.

To enable our scouts to provide us with a workable evaluation, we have formulated a rating scale from which a player can be categorized. The scale rates each footballer in relation to a norm. We have found that the five-step scale works exceptionally well. It is simple, yet effective.

EVALUATING SPEED		EVALUATING REACTIONS	
Rating	*Description*	*Rating*	*Description*
1 ——	Fast	1 ——	Excellent
2 ——	Above Average	2 ——	Above Average
3 ——	Average	3 ——	Average
4 ——	Below Average	4 ——	Below Average
5 ——	Slow	5 ——	Poor

Those that might be critical of rating would argue that whenever using a subjective method, validity of the results is restricted. There is a degree of logic here, but this system at least forces judgment upon the scout. It seems reasonable that the educated opinion of someone who knows football is better than no rating at all.

WHAT ABOUT THE ENDS?

The function of defensive ends has a great bearing on the type of pass coverage used. Ends who are used to pick up the near back, or flow to the flat when flood action appears, add to the potential coverage by serving as pass defenders. Without question, utilization of ends strengthens the total perimeter of a secondary. Teams that exhibit this form of coverage generally do not put the big rush on the passer, thus allowing time to throw the ball.

By scouting responsibilities of defensive ends, a good idea of the type of passing plays that will be successful can be determined. As a general rule, if ends drop off, deeper pass patterns should go, since a limited rush provides needed time to throw the bomb.

If defensive ends are stationed in a walk-away position (off line), to take away the look-in pass and allow coverage of the flat, a good strategy is to attack the flanks with a sprint-out or roll-out pass. This play places ends in a vulnerable position since they cannot adequately pressure the sprint-out, nor can they defend against the pass.

LINEBACKERS—THE KEY

Many factors need attention when scouting linebacker play. The depth at which a linebacker plays, his speed, size, agility, and reactions, all should be observed. Together, these capacities relate to his range or potential covering ability. There are linebackers who can defend the deep hook zone (twelve yards deep), while others have trouble covering as little as five yards in depth. As stated in an earlier chapter, a short passing game depends upon the ability of linebackers. Knowing the basic characteristics of these players dictates the kind of short patterns to be used.

One other consideration to be made when evaluating linebackers is whether they blitz and, if so, how often, on what down and distance. Teams that gamble for the big play by popping linebackers leave themselves vulnerable for a check-off, look-in, near-back, screen, or any other quickly developing pass play. When scouting linebackers who do a lot of red-dogging, tendencies related to field position or down and distance will show up, allowing good insight into when to expect the pressure.

DETECTING WEAKNESS WITH A CHART

A very good method of evaluating a team's pass defense potential is by charting all patterns used against them in previous games. A form we call Chart of Zone Responsibility and Pass Completions is used for this purpose and is shown in Figure 13-3. Note that the form divides the secondary into five specific zones. This measuring technique also provides for a record of completed and incompleted passes in each zone, as well as the types of pattern run by the opposition. Depth and course of each pattern can be drawn on this form.

The specific objective of this form is to determine breakdowns in the enemy's secondary and kinds of patterns that

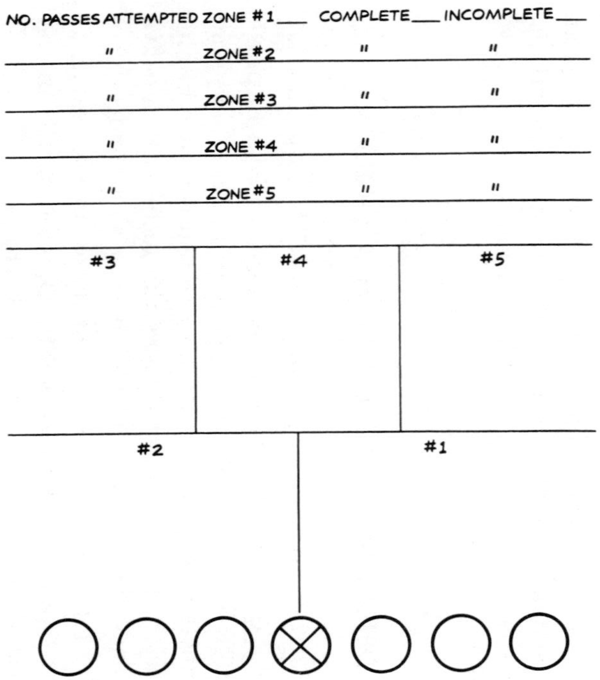

DEF. SEC. ALWT.	PATTERN DESCRIPTION	COMPL. YDS. GND.	INCOMPLETE WHY	INTERCEPTED WHY	COMMENT

RECEIVER AND PATTERN TENDENCY CHART

FIGURE 13-4

NO. PASSES ATTEMPTED ZONE #1 ____ COMPLETE ____ INCOMPLETE ____

" ZONE #2 " "

" ZONE #3 " "

" ZONE #4 " "

" ZONE #5 " "

#1 #2 #3 #4 #5

CHART OF ZONE RESPONSIBILITY AND PASS COMPLETIONS

FIGURE 13-3

would be successful. This chart can serve as a guide to determine whether the short or deep passing game might be most effective. It also points out what type and depth of patterns to run within the various zones.

RECEIVER AND PATTERN TENDENCY CHART

A very valuable form is a Receiver and Pattern Tendency Chart, shown in Figure 13-4. This chart serves as a record of what patterns have been successful by other teams against the opposition. It also points out the type of defensive secondary alignment used—three-deep, four-deep, monster. There are places on the form to note if a pass is completed or an interception made. This information helps determine which defender is getting beat and why. In addition, this chart allows for comments related to the ability of individuals, secondarymen, and the performance of the entire secondary. In short, the Receiver and Pattern Tendency Chart condenses the play of an opponent's pass defense by evaluating a team's effectiveness against other clubs.

SCOUTING PAYS OFF

Scouting to observe, determine, and analyze the enemy's ability to defend against your aerial attack is a vital phase of constructing one's game plan. A sound passing offense, geared to taking advantage of an opponent's weaknesses, can overcome any defensive alignment.

Do a good job of looking over an opposition's pass defense. Knowledge of an opponent's personnel potential and position placement will promote confidence and aggressiveness in your team.

Yes, scouting produces dividends—in completions and victories!

14

Developing Effective Quarterback Strategy

Using the forward pass in an offense is a must, but equally important is developing a method of calling appropriate pass plays at the correct time. We do not contend that there is a flawless method of calling for the pass, but certainly there are some guidelines to consider. It is conceded that personnel, weather conditions, down and distance, score of game, time remaining, and other elements influence the type and amount of passing plays used in a game. Still there are some elementary factors to consider when selecting plays.

A concept that has proven effective over the years is to throw whenever possible on first down. Furthermore, attempt to use a pass play that is designed to produce a score. Play-action passes are particularly effective on first down. Another example of this might be an out-and-up pattern or hook-and-go pattern. If the play is successful, the team receives a tremendous psychological lift. If not, there still remain two or possibly three downs (depending on field position) to work on the first down. If on first downs a team has been throwing a lot, then when a running play is called on first down, it tends to go quite well.

On second down, if the distance is still ten yards to go, it is suggested that a pass play to get a first down be used. Hook passes, look-ins, square-outs, hook and slides, cross-in or cross-out patterns, all can get yardage needed for the first down. If a first down is not gained, then again it is necessary to come up with something to keep the drive going. A completion now becomes imperative and consideration should lean toward getting the ball to the best receiver, or perhaps calling the pattern that most often succeeds. If a pass is not called, a running play that can get good yardage should be used.

There is less variation in choice of third down plays. If the distance for a first down is not great, the pass becomes obvious. We have had good success on this play by showing the defense pro type sets and running the draw or Sally Rand. Passes that are extremely reliable in a third down and five situation are out, cross-in, Zorro, hook, hook slide-in, and hook slide-out. If distance to go is under five yards, the sprint-out pass, near-back pass, or look-in are especially sound calls. If the third down situation is short yardage and a running play is desired, normally the off-tackle power is a good solution. A longer third down yardage situation might call for a sweep or reverse play.

FIELD POSITION

Closely related to play selection is field position. When a team is operating on a hashmark, the kind of pattern should be one that will not be hampered by available room. While many teams use sideline patterns, or patterns that break out to the short side of the field, it nevertheless restricts the way the pattern will be run and when the ball will be thrown.

The area of the field best suited for passing lies between your own forty and the other team's forty yard line. This zone provides the offense with the opportunity to use any of its pass patterns. This field position does not limit the passing game, and is particularly advantageous for throwing the bomb. There is room to throw deep, and an interception of a deep pass in this field position serves as well as a punt. Therefore, it is good logic to throw deep on occasions when the ball rests between the forties.

TYPES OF COVERAGE

An offense, while passing against a zone or man-to-man defensive secondary, must be concerned with separate specific problems. Coverage must be considered. Against a zone defense, the strategy generally is either to flood a given zone with more receivers than the defender of that zone can cover, or to clear a zone by sending a receiver deep and running a second man into the same zone with a shorter pattern. A team that uses man-for-man coverage presents a different problem for a passing offense. Cutting patterns that allow receivers to cross are often successful against the man-for-man defense.

Knowing the type of pattern or play to run at a given time depends upon the previously mentioned factors. There is no cut-and-dried way to select the best play to use at a specific time. We ask our quarterbacks to learn and use the slogan, *Be conservative when ahead—gamble when behind.*

The longer the yardage, the bigger or more wide-open the play used, is a general rule of thumb when considering types of pass plays. Tell your quarterback to think big when it is a big play. There are situations that are particularly good for given patterns or plays. They are created by the score of the game, field position, down and distance, weather conditions, or type of personnel playing. These situations give rise to a need for rules to help play-calling strategy. One teaching aid to help instill in our quarterbacks some important concepts of play-calling, is what we call the Suggested Ten Rules of Generalship:

1) Always call a pattern that will get a first down when a first down is needed.

2) When deep in your own territory and a third down situation arises with more than four yards to go, throw the bomb.

3) Throw the long pass immediately after a psychological change. For example, when you intercept a pass, run a punt for long yardage, recover a fumble, etc.

4) Use less dangerous plays when ahead in game. Gamble when behind.

5) Use play-action passes when there is a short yardage situation.

6) Call some new patterns, formations, plays, early in game. Rely on basic bread and butter plays as game progresses.

7) Be careful about throwing on fourth down unless late in game or inside opposition's forty yard line.

8) When third down and long yardage situation prevails, don't be afraid to run with the ball. Use Sally Rand, draw, trap, options, sweep, and reverse.

9) Show your opponent a different formation late in second quarter if opportunity presents itself. Give him something to think about at half time.

10) Use sets that place your best receiver against the poorest defender whenever possible.

There are some specific elements that deserve mention for choosing appropriate plays. These factors should be considered in relation to evaluating conditions prior to selection of a play. Overlooking any one of these factors could result in an unsuccessful play. We ask our signal callers to memorize these rules, which we refer to as the Ten Golden Laws of Play-Calling:

1) Can this play get a first down or score?

2) Will play succeed against the present defensive alignment?

3) Is condition of field appropriate for play?

4) What is time remaining and score of game?

5) Which play has been most successful thus far in game?

6) If this play fails, what other play will succeed?

7) Has this play been properly set up?

8) Do we have good field position?

9) From which set will the play best succeed?

10) Is most suitable back being used?

Selecting a play based solely on the aforementioned facts is not advisable. There are intangibles that must be considered. Such things as imagination in play-calling can change the entire outcome of a game, because the unexpected or wide-open play is more difficult to defend against. This is particularly true when a big play is called when the routine play is expected. Why not throw the bomb on the second down and one yard to go situation? Why not on the first and five yards play? Why not pass on fourth and second when it is not a punting situation?

As suggested previously, there is no such thing as a correct play. Any play that succeeds is a good play. A specific play that excels one week may not in another game. Rather than having fixed rules for determining what play should be selected, it is advisable to follow certain *guidelines* as listed earlier. But by no means should these be construed as dictatorial!

RECOGNIZING DEFENSIVE ALIGNMENT

All defenses are stronger at one point or another—and in every defense there are weaknesses. The job of the signal caller is to recognize this and adjust his play-calling accordingly. Certain defenses can prevent specific plays from function-

FIGURE 14–1   WEAKNESSES OF 6–1

Suggested patterns:
Near-back pass to flanker side
Look-in
Throw-back pass
Hook
Cross-in

WEAKNESSES OF SPLIT 6

Suggested patterns:
Sideline
Hook
Look-in to split end
Near-back pass
Flood action
Sprint-out play

FIGURE 14–2   WEAKNESSES OF 5–3

Suggested patterns:
Flood action
Sprint-out play
Deep

WEAKNESSES OF 5–4

Suggested patterns:
  Near-back pass to set side flanker
  Throw-back pass off sprint-out action
  Sideline or square-out
  Cross-out

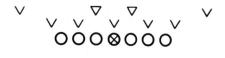

FIGURE 14–3   WEAKNESSES OF 6–2 REGULAR

Suggested patterns:
  Look-in
  Cross-in
  Any flood action variety
  Sprint-out play

WEAKNESSES OF 6–2 WIDE

Suggested patterns:
  Near-back pass
  Sideline or square-out
  Flood action
  Sprint-out play

ing, while at the same time, they present opportunities for other plays. We feel there are three simple aspects of defensive recognition a signal caller should concern himself with: How many linebackers are there and where are they located? What are the stations of the deep backs? What type of coverage is the secondary using?

Figures 14-1 to 14-3 show defensive sets and suggested patterns for these defenses. This form can also be used to note variations a team is using in their basic defense. General comments can be added regarding defense or offensive thinking.

THIRTEEN CHANCES A TEAM GETS

During a given game, a team gets the opportunity to score at least thirteen times. That is to say, there is an average exchange of the ball thirteen times per game. Games are not won or lost because a team does not have the opportunity to score! Rather, contests are won or lost according to what happens after a team acquires the ball. Mistakes made when your team has possession of the pigskin is where you lose *every* game that is lost. Victories result from a sound offense based on well-executed plays.

POSSESSION OF THE BALL IS EVERYTHING!

Maintaining ball control determines the success of any offense. The old concept that the enemy can't score if they don't have the ball is as valid today as it was yesterday. The team that has the football the most times in a game simply has more opportunity to get it across the goal line. Therefore, a large portion of play-calling is choosing the play that may best keep a drive going.

We do not contend that it is not sound football to go for the long gain. To the contrary, a passing team must be able to produce the big play. However, percentages are with the offense on the shorter yardage play. Chances are generally greater of completing the hook or look-in pass over the flag or streak pattern.

Obviously there are a number of reasons for the aforementioned fact—but pass protection and quick execution are prime reasons. On the deeper pass route, pass protection blocking must exist longer, adding a variable to the play. Patterns that take time also allow the defensive secondary to react and recover if necessary, while the rapidly developing play gives the defense little opportunity to read or diagnose plays.

KEEPING ACES IN THE HOLE

It matters not, how many yards a play gained in previous contests. Each week there is a new team exemplifying different ability, philosophy, and tactics. What counts is what success given plays have on game day. Predicting the probability of a play's success can be aided by certain factors. Among these elements are sequence, surprise, and modification.

Sequence

It is unrealistic to expect a play to succeed with regularity unless it has been properly set up. Big plays are ones that are used at the right time and place. Sequence is the order of succession into which plays are grouped. The best play for the appropriate time is dependent upon it being in the correct place of sequence. For example, the play-action pass should not be used until the play it is related to has been used several times.

Surprise

Surprise can be the most important essential in play selection. The best time to use a particular play is when the opponent is not expecting it. A good way to create surprise is to put yourself in the position of the enemy, anticipate what you would do in their situation, and then do something extremely different. Surprise means doing something that was not done the week before, in a similar situation. Surprise comes from deception. An example is using a running play in a passing situation, or vice versa.

Modification

With the quality of scouting today, teams go into games well-informed and thoroughly versed on the opposition. Therefore, a club that does not modify its offense somewhat each week becomes stereotyped. Scouting these clubs unveils tendencies. Any change from the normal alignment in an offense can cause defensive confusion and eliminate offensive tendencies. Deviations should be made, particularly with respect to basic sets, in priority to specific plays. However, formation or play change will keep an offense explosive. As long as these modifications are kept simple they should not hinder the offense. For example, by moving one back around in the formation and keeping everyone else intact, a new look has been created.

Whether it be sequence, surprise, or modification in an offense, what is important is that these elements be *considered.* Each game presents a separate and new problem which must dictate what will be your ace in the hole.

PSYCHOLOGY IN PLAY-CALLING

There is a tremendous amount of psychology to play-calling. Having a sound play, and the proper situation to execute it, is not enough. The quarterback and, above all, the players must believe the play called will work. When there is confidence, almost anything will go.

A task for the coach and, for that matter, the field general, is to convince players of the potency of each play that is called. This can be done through the poise and self-reliance a signal caller displays. Players evaluate the attitude of the quarterback. If he demonstrates calmness and vocal command, footballers will generally be receptive and aggressive in nature. It is a good idea for signal callers to learn that, *when important calls are made, over-emphasize confidence in the play.* We say to our quarterback, "Be direct, be positive, be right."

Allowing your field general to take an active part in team meetings, leadership during practice, and providing him with a great deal of responsibility, undoubtedly will encourage a secure feeling among the players. It is not logical or realistic to expect a quarterback to excel under pressure if he is not trusted to do so in practice and at other times. Invest hours, energy, and faith in your quarterback. It will pay off when needed the most.

THE QUARTERBACK HANDBOOK

Teaching your philosophy of play selection can be greatly aided by using a Quarterback Manual. This teaching aid should stress the WHY as well as the HOW. Any signal caller will be much more effective if he is aware of *why* various components of the game need emphasis, must be used at given times, and relate to total offense. Once the quarterback knows the *why* aspect of a philosophy, he will be ready to accept the *how* phase of learning.

This handbook must outline these two concepts of generalship. The *why* and *how* of offensive football can be broken down into universally adaptable purposes. These aims are designed to provide quarterbacks with their duties, responsibilities and, as stated previously, a solid knowledge of system and ideology. Included in this teaching booklet ought to be information on:

1) Statement of offensive philosophy.
2) Principles of play selection.
3) Breakdown of opponent's defensive trends and personnel.
4) Evaluation of own players' ability (backs and reserves).
5) Poor weather condition tips—why.
6) When to gamble—when to be conservative—why.
7) Why play sequence.
8) Beating the block—why and how.
9) Using field position—why and how.
10) Down and distance effect on play calling—why.

In addition to the above mentioned criteria, we like to include in this notebook some personal data for our quarterbacks. This manual may be of particular significance to a field general in the off-season. Meeting with the quarterbacks in the months preceding the season and discussing these attributes will pay big dividends. Subjects that we stress are:

1) The role of a quarterback.

2) What constitutes leadership—why is it important?

3) Off-season preparation—physical and mental.

4) Ways to build pride and enthusiasm within squad.

5) Learn complete offense thoroughly.

If the handbook is a loose-leaf notebook, naturally it will be easy to keep up to date. The three-hole type binder has served our needs well.

KNOW THE ZONES

A football field can be partitioned into five zones, which serves to classify what type and where various passing plays should be run. Our contention is that certain patterns will be more successful if used in specific positions on the battlefield. Factors that influence passing and dictate what kind of routes can be run within zones are:

1) System of defense being employed by opposition:

    A) Number of men on line of scrimmage.

    B) Type of secondary coverage.

    C) Stunting or non-stunting defense.

2) Strength and ability of opponent.

3) On hashmark or middle of field.

4) Time remaining in game.

5) Weather conditions.

6) Ability of team.

We use a Passing Zone Chart (Figure 14-4) to help determine the types of patterns we anticipate using in a game. Information placed on the chart is based on scouting reports and knowledge of our own personnel and system. We give our

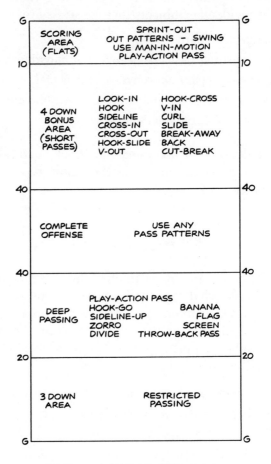

FIGURE 14–4 PASSING ZONE CHART

quarterbacks a copy of this chart every Monday. In a meeting later in the week, the information on the form should be discussed with the quarterback.

BEAT THE STUNTING DEFENSE

Because some teams today have defenses that are not standard in alignment, due to movement on or before snap of the ball, teams must be able to counter this action. If linemen and linebackers change position, blocking rules are distorted and the offense generally bogs down. Therefore a necessary retaliation for this system of defense is plays that are functionable against a changing defense. Running plays that are normally successful are wedges and plays designed to run right at the defense. We have found too that the near-back, screen, and look-in passes are extremely effective in overcoming this obstacle. Having an audible system that can call for these special plays or patterns at the line of scrimmage is the best solution to this defensive approach.

LOOK OUT FOR THE POOR CALL

It only takes one bad play selection to end a march or prevent a touchdown. Only when all aspects of the game plan and guidelines for play calling have been considered, can mistakes in play selection be decreased. The play that will often kill an offensive drive is likely to be the one that seems logical, but it can be eliminated through knowledge of the opposition. This statement can be verified if one will recall that games have been won, not lost, if a certain play had not occurred. In short, poor play calling is the result of bad judgment. Since all judgment is based on knowledge, proper selection should not be a difficult chore.

WHAT CONSTITUTES GENERALSHIP?

This chapter on generalship tries to transmit a variety of criticisms as well as some positive suggestions pertinent to play-calling. Of the material presented, it is hoped that two themes stand out—knowing *what* to do and *when* to do it. A good quarterback will reflect the ideology of the coaching staff. Thus our job as coaches is to inspire our field general with a sound philosophy of offensive football.

If any of the thoughts offered here are of service to you, this chapter has accomplished its objective and perhaps helped eliminate losing through poor play selection.

15

How Putting the Ball
in the Air
Affects Defense

Current defensive alignment is somewhat ineffective against the forward pass. The use of flanker backs, split ends, and men-in-motion has forced defenses to cover the entire field rather than one part of it. The hypothesis that larger areas of defensive coverage hamper effectiveness certainly has merit. These detached men have much more room to maneuver because the defensive secondary has an increased area to defend. This is of particular significance on individual routes, when one pass-catcher challenges a single defender. The end result is a higher percentage of pass completions.

USING THE SIDELINE AS A DEFENDER

Since offensive trends have been toward spreading personnel, theories of defense have changed to compensate for this tendency. One of these changes involves position placement of the defensive secondary. Because of the amount of running room a receiver has, it is impossible for a defender to take away both the quick inside and outside patterns.

A current method of accomplishing this object is for the defensive man to maintain an inside position on the offensive man. This alignment will cut off quick inside patterns, seemingly leaving only the outside vulnerable. It should be remembered that if the offensive man is detached from the main body of the offense, this distance from the sideline cannot be too great. In addition, a route to the outside of the spread man is a long pass, allowing more time for coverage.

An inside position taken on a receiver by a secondaryman will vary in yardage dependent upon the exact distance from the sideline and the amount of split. A good rule is the longer the split, the more pronounced the inside position. A defensive halfback playing an end split fifteen yards might take a position of three yards inside the detached man. While a man flanked but eight yards may require an inside position of less than one yard. A very short split may mean an aligning position to the inside shoulder of the offensive man.

In all these defensive personnel placements, the sideline serves as another defender. This is so because the sideline restricts the distance a receiver has to run his pattern. In reality the sideline is like having another man on defense.

CHANGING ALIGNMENT

We feel the forward pass continues to revolutionize defensive football. It is feasible that in the very near future the passing game in college and high school teams will confine a defense to some philosophy of seven-man coverage. With an increased emphasis on throwing the ball, defenses will have to consider the best way they can defend against the pass. Professional football has adapted and perfected the four-man line as the way to defend against the forward pass. Defensive alignment of high school and college football is beginning to change as teams are placing less men on the line of scrimmage. The days of eight, seven, and perhaps six-man lines are nearly over.

Without question, the concept of defending against the

forward pass with the big rush is still the best way to throttle a pass offense. However, today it is the linebackers who add this pressure to the passer, rather than six or seven linemen. This is done by blitzing these defenders on given situations.

Decreasing the number of players on the line of scrimmage allows better coverage of receivers. Only a few years ago, flat passes, such as near-back, delayed, or screen, were almost impossible for linebackers or halfbacks to cover because the total of pass defenders consisted of four to five men. Since there were six individuals elgible to receive the ball, it was difficult to defend against this form of pass. The only reason teams were not beaten badly by these types of passes was that offenses did not really utilize them.

Football today does use these passes and other complicated forms of pass patterns. Thus defenses have changed and will continue to change to meet the challenge of the previously mentioned passing philosophies. This change undoubtedly forces teams into professional-type defenses.

EFFECT UPON PERSONNEL

Increased stress on throwing the ball is not only affecting defenses, but the type of personnel that plays defense. There must be a greater emphasis today on mobility and reaction than ever before. Defensive halfbacks and safeties have to defend against the sprinter who is flanked out and called an end or backer. These secondarymen must cover receivers for a longer period of time than their predecessors. With fewer men on the line of scrimmage, and play-action passes and sprint-out maneuvers, receivers can use multiple-cut patterns and techniques that are almost impossible to cover.

Linebackers are often placed in the difficult situation of covering a receiver who may be much faster. A linebacker today must be both quick and tall. Playing in a defensive secondary, you need all the qualities of those who played these positions a few years ago, plus the ability to play pass defense better than it has ever been played before. In addition, many defenses attempt to cover a man-in-motion with a linebacker, which is again extremely difficult.

For the individual, the passing game has created physical problems as well as mental pressure. Defensive specialists are confronted with a wide variety of sets or formations that require a lot of knowledge of the opposition's ability and potential. Certain sets should be defended against in a given manner, as should specific individuals.

Because of the above mentioned factors, defensive units need more than one form of coverage to compensate. These problems are being multiplied further as the passing game becomes more intricate each year.

POSITIONING INFLUENCED

The danger of the forward pass, like the foot of a good punter, is forcing defensive secondaries to be physically and mentally "deep conscious." This fear has affected defensive containment particularly. When there is concern for preventing completions and stress on eliminating the long pass, containing the running game also becomes difficult. Secondarymen cannot be expected to stop a running attack at the line of scrimmage and at the same time not get beat deep by a receiver. Thus, defensive secondaries are becoming more specialized for defending against the pass and less qualified to restrict the running game. The end result is that emphasis and success of throwing the pigskin is influencing defensive football and causing change.

ALTERS PREPARATION

The effect of passing upon defense is particularly evident in the type of practice sessions that prevail in football today. Practices are geared to include a large portion of time defending against the throwing game. Stress must be placed on adequately defending each and every aspect of passing if an aerial attack is to be stopped. This kind of emphasis requires a great deal of specialization, which in turn leads to involved, lengthy drills perfecting these specialties. The team that recognizes and defends against the forward pass is far less prone to lose contests than one that does not prepare for the passing game.

LINEMEN PLAY

It is generally known and accepted that the best way to stop a pass offense is through the rush. If this be true, teams that advocate a soft or controlling defense are at a great disadvantage when matched against a throwing club. Because we believe this concept, we predict defensive thinking and philosophy will change. The pressure system of defense will soon replace the wait-and-see or keying technique for linemen. If this change does not occur, look for the drop-back method of passing to dominate offensive football.

DEFENDING AGAINST THE LOOK-IN

Perhaps the biggest innovation the aerial game has adopted is the look-in pass to a detached player. This pattern in itself has revolutionized the entire concept of pass defense. No longer can a zone coverage supply adequate protection. A good receiver from a split position, running a look-in pattern, is literally unstoppable, unless special consideration is given to the play. Therefore, defenses have established methods to compensate for the offensive advantage. Such measures as man-to-man coverage and man-and-a-half coverage have become standard procedure for guarding against this deadly pass. Defensive secondarymen are required to play very close to a receiver, preventing him from getting the quick inside position.

Placing a man on the head of an isolated receiver, or slightly inside on the line of scrimmage, is another trend in defending the look-in. This technique, however, is costly to the defense. It forces them to use two men against one, cutting down on the number of defensive personnel defending against the complete offense.

NEW TERMINOLOGY

The passing game has had great impact on modern football, not only on defense, but also on football terminology. Words like *cornerbacks, wings, inside safeties, free safeties, strong* and *weak safeties, monsters, rovers,* and *bandits* were nonexistent a few years ago. In addition, various types of coverage have created names to identify the methods of defending against the pass. Many teams have even labeled individual defensive players to better identify them and their responsibilities.

A PROGNOSIS

Unless the present rules of play are altered drastically, field narrowed and shortened, or the football itself changed in shape, this great American sport will be controlled by the offense. Putting the ball in the air is the main reason for this evolution—it provides thrust and explosiveness, the very essence of offense. A new kind of football is emerging and defense has fallen behind in importance.

16

How to Build
Your Passing Game
in Practice

A team's success depends upon its practice. What is done in practice is tested on game day. A passing team must continually work to perfect its throwing game. We believe the difference between winning and losing is a little more practice. Passing should become the most important phase of every session. The team has to know this fact and support it. If footballers believe in throwing the ball, they will enjoy playing football. *Young men who like the game are prospective winners.* Therefore, a coach's primary objective in teaching and stressing aerial football is creating practices that are conducive to learning and fun.

MAKING PRACTICE FUN

Coaches vary in their opinions regarding how to establish a productive atmosphere. We hold the philosophy that there are some specific approaches to develop a learning environment. The tempo or climate of practice is reflective of teaching methods and objectives. Practices that hold the interests of footballers will aid in the motivation process. With the limited attention span of many kids, the interest factor restricts what can be done in a given practice. To counteract mental limitations of players, our coaching staff plans the workouts with five things in mind. These five vital planning devices to combat mental fatigue are: (1) limiting length of practice; (2) using change-of-pace tactics; (3) allowing time off; (4) keeping enthusiasm high; and (5) maintaining a variety of fast-moving activities.

Limiting length of practice

One of the surest ways to develop boredom is conducting long, extensive workouts. When determining the length of practice, factors such as the day of the week, opponent, and time of the year are considered. As a general rule, however, we do not feel any practice should exceed two hours. The first and last practices of the week might be considerably shorter, while the middle sessions serve as work days.

Using change-of-pace tactics

As a session gets well along, players tire of the daily routine. If this occurs, practice becomes dull and meaningless. Left unchecked, this situation can become serious. Alleviating this problem can be done by varying the drills and activities of practice. There are many drills or procedures that can accomplish the same objectives that the routine drills do.

Adding activities that encourage fun helps players' attitudes. A swimming party or basketball game after a short practice can raise spirits. Touch football (backs vs. line) is fun and a good way to start a practice. Relays of many sorts can provide stimulation. All of the aforementioned help maintain hustle and build morale.

Allowing time off

There are times in every practice session when both players and coaches need a day off. Normally, this concession comes late in the campaign, when the wear and tear of mental and physical strain begin to be apparent. A day off after a big win is also sometimes a good policy.

The value of a rest may be more psychological than anything else. Regardless, our experiences indicate that the kids come back after a layoff with increased pep and vigor. Mondays have proven best for this purpose.

Keeping enthusiasm high

It is necessary sometimes to rely on gimics as a means to create enthusiasm. Allowing the players a Hat Day, where they can wear any type of headpiece they desire, is fun for the kids. On this day we put the team in sweat suits and do no more than throw the football around.

A second enthusiasm-producer can be a Mom's Day. This event allows mothers to attend a practice and discuss mutual concerns. We generally hold Mom's Day on a day after a game or on Monday. At this activity refreshments are served by mothers to footballers immediately following the workout.

Still another successful method of relieving tensions is through a Press Day. All of us like our picture taken and name mentioned in the newspaper. This is the greatest form of recognition players receive. They want and need it. Therefore, inviting the press and radio to a practice once each year is worthwhile. The school yearbook and school paper can be asked to participate. We have gone so far as to ask friends to come out with their cameras—anything to make the kids feel important. It is a good idea to have one's wife out shooting pictures of those players not getting much attention. It doesn't matter whether or not she uses film. The important thing is to supply each kid with attention.

A technique that has proven effective for us is having Film Days. At these festivities we culminate our practice early and retire to a classroom where we look at a good football film. It may be a college game or a pro contest. The important thing is that it is entertaining. We have also taken the most poorly executed plays of previous games and pointed out how bad we can look without even trying. It is important here that this be done in fun, without levying blame on individuals.

Maintaining a variety of fast-moving activities

The four above methods of making practice fun all contribute to achieving variety in activities. Variety encourages spirit, keeps morale high, and takes the drudgery from workouts.

WHAT IS STRESSED IN PRACTICE
PAYS DIVIDENDS IN THE GAME

Football is like life—you do best in what you work at the hardest. It takes effort to do a big job. There is a direct correlation between winning games through the air and the amount of emphasis placed on the passing game in practice. It stands to reason that if a passing attack makes up a good part of the offense, proportional time must be given to this aspect in each practice.

Coaches must have the philosophy that if fifty percent of practice time is spent on perfecting the passing attack, about that same amount of success will prevail. The club that devotes sixty percent of practice time to passing will reflect that figure. The more time given to the throwing game, the better passing team you will have. If this theory is not accepted, the passing game will not be effective.

Organizing a practice schedule developed around the forward pass is most important. Players recognize the emphasis placed on passing and relate its prominence. An explanation of this is, when practice begins by stressing pass offense and ends in the same vein, evidence of its importance is obvious.

WARM-UP FOR PRACTICE

There are warm-up techniques that help prepare players for their daily workouts. The function of these procedures is to warm all muscles and develop specific skills related to the pass offense. To the quarterback it means getting his arm ready to throw. Receivers concentrate on their legs and arms, while interior linemen work on their shoulders and necks. All these attentions are directed at making each and every player cognizant of his needs.

Warm-ups are done in two stages. Beginning when footballers reach the field, simple stretching and loosening up exercises are done individually. In phase two, players do special, pre-determined drills stressing the aerial game. (These drills are all diagrammed and explained in Chapter 17).

By dividing the field into areas, various phases of specialization can be worked on according to needs. Linemen report to Area C for pass protection blocking work, while backs go to either Area A or B, according to assignment. (Note that in Figure 16-2 the football field is broken into divisions of specialization.)

THE PRACTICE SCHEDULE CARD

A very effective way to break down a practice schedule is by using a 4x5 card (see Figure 16-1). The Practice Schedule Card provides a place to write the time a given activity will begin and end, name of drill, and coach responsible. When each coach has and uses this card, all know exactly when and

TIME	DRILL	COACH
COMMENT		

FIGURE 16–1   PRACTICE SCHEDULE CARD

where a particular drill is being conducted, as well as who is directing. These cards act as a record for future evaluation. Being pocket size, they are easily handled and ideal for use on the field. We run off 750 cards at the beginning of the season, which gets us through the year.

COACHING STATIONS AND RESPONSIBILITIES

Coaching football is a continuing battle against time. When coaches have specific responsibilities and teaching stations from which to coach, better utilization of the staff and practice time will result. With the many intricate aspects of football, practices must be highly planned and organized. The strength, knowledge, and ability of each coach should be called upon.

We like to break practice into three phases: the pre-practice, regular, and post-practice sessions. Each of these parts serves to accomplish certain objectives and varies in length accordingly. Coaches are assigned teaching stations that will allow for the best execution of their specialized responsibility. The number and kind of stations are dependent upon

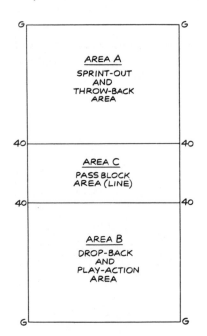

FIGURE 16–2   PRACTICE FIELD

Coaching Stations and Areas of Emphasis

the size of your staff and practice field area. Figure 16-2 points out how a typical practice field might be mapped out to provide for specialized work in practice.

A suggested length for the three parts of practice are:

Pre-practice	20 min.
Regular session	1 hr. 15 min.
Post-practice	10 min.

The duration of these phases of practice may vary with respect to the time of year and needs at hand. Early season may warrant a longer pre-practice, since here is where much of the work with individuals can be done. The latter portion of the campaign may feature a more extensive post-practice session, because this is when correction of faulty techniques or skills is stressed. Our coaching duties have been broken down into one coach for each group of ends, interior linemen, backs and quarterbacks.

METHODS OF TEACHING THE PASSING GAME

Pre-practice

In a period that lasts from 20 to 30 minutes, in which all players concentrate on passing game-fundamentals and skills, linemen work on pass protection blocking, receivers on catching passes and improving moves, and passers perfect their throwing. While the passing game is being stressed during this phase of practice, pass defense is emphasized.

Regular session

Usually making up about two-thirds of the entire practice time, in this period the units, teams, or groups are brought together for team development work. This could be dummy scrimmage, semi-live, or full contact. Stop-the-clock and two-minute drills should also be taught during this session. About an hour and fifteen minutes is spent on this aspect of practice.

Post-practice

At the conclusion of regular practice we have found it profitable to devote extra time to facets of our aerial attack that need attention. This is a good opportunity to work on screen passes and other passing plays that are not regularly stressed. This ten-minute portion of practice is used to do isometric exercises which we feel help promote the passing game.

SPECIAL WORK WITH QUARTERBACKS

We have found that the level of excellence displayed by a quarterback will normally parallel the quality of play demonstrated by the team. (Or, a club is about as good as its quarterback.) With stress today on sprinting or rolling out, the importance of a field general is becoming increasingly significant. Consequently our quarterbacks are expected to spend more time in practice and meetings than any other player. As indicated earlier, practice is separated into three phases. Pre-practice allows time for giving the quarterback special attention.

When our quarterbacks reach the field, they involve themselves in several warm-up and fundamental drills which concentrate on perfecting basic skills of execution: exchange and various passing drills, sprint-out and drop-back techniques. These drills are referred to in Chapter 17 as Feel the Ball, Look at Me, Form Drill, Circle Drill, Loosen Up, Time Drill, Play Catch, One Knee Down, Throwing On Time, Set Up by Count, Bring the Ball Over, Read Pressure, and Line Drill. During execution, a coach can work very closely with the quarterbacks on little things not allowed for during practice time. Attention should be given to fundamentals.

TIME ALLOTMENT FOR SPECIFIC
PHASES OF PASS OFFENSE

Implementing an aerial game in practice is dependent upon adequate attention to all facets of pass offense. Since we advocate four general types of throwing, it is necessary to devote time and energy to perfecting each. A review of a recent year's practice schedule indicates time spent specifically on elements of the passing game. The four components of the throwing game are the drop-back, sprint-out, play-action, and throw-back plays. Time allotted to these phases of offense has been twenty, ten, five, and five minutes, respectively. Preparing for specific teams sometimes requires greater emphasis on one or more of the components.

A method to insure that all parts of the pass offense, as well as patterns, are being adhered to daily is through the use of a chart. This establishes a running record of when the above-mentioned aspects of this aerial attack are used. We have a Daily Pass Pattern Check Chart as shown in Figure 16-3. This chart reminds quarterbacks of patterns they might occasionally forget. And, in addition, it encourages passers to throw daily to all receivers and all routes.

By keeping the chart on the field and having the quarterbacks check it, specific pass routes will never be overlooked. A good technique for utilizing this form is to set it next to the

FIGURE 16–3

PASS PATTERN CHECK CHART

PATTERN	FORM-ATION	DAY OF WEEK				
		M	T	W	T	F

center, on the ground in passing drills, so that the quarter-back can see it each time he comes up to begin the drill.

USE THE STOPWATCH

If preparation for a game is competitive and realistic in nature, footballers will respond more readily. Two basic approaches to making practice activities competitive are pitting players against players or players against time. Since it is impossible to always allow physical contact while preparing for a contest, working to defeat the clock is logical.

When players are timed, they tend to supply the little extra effort it takes to make a play go. They will have pride in themselves and work to better their time of execution. As football is essentially a game involving execution against time, coaching with a stopwatch is a way of injecting into practice the natural pressure of a game.

If various aspects of practice are designed to function with the aid of a coach and a timing device, sessions will be conducive to meaningful performance. Therefore use a stopwatch and witness the positive results.

GO LIVE!

Working on the components of pass offense, as stressed earlier, is a prime requisite for success. Another ingredient that will aid in bringing about this result is executing live, as much of practice as possible. Drilling against people, like against a watch, makes practice realistic.

All phases of the aerial game profit from execution of talents live. Receivers who catch the ball with defenders around them in practice, will have no problem doing the same come game time. Passers asked to throw under the pressure of a rush are unlikely to fold when real action starts. Linemen blocking live, moving targets in practice, will be better qualified to meet the demands during a contest.

While we are the first to admit it is impossible to go live

every minute of practice every day, nevertheless a good portion of practice time can and should be devoted to some form of contact. To insure that enough work is done live each week, we break practice down into about fifty percent live work and fifty percent non-contact. Live practice drilling is classified into full contact, semi-contact, and initial hit.

Making up the full contact phase of practice is: scrimmage, controlled scrimmage, blocking, and various other live drills. Semi-contact includes activities and drills that allow contact to be made by some team members while it restricts others. Initial hit refers to contact being made, but with no follow-through. Non-contact work is activity placing players against bags, other teaching aids, or nothing. This type of practice serves three objectives: it is a good warm-up procedure, sound for teaching something new, and excellent to polish an attack. The value of this form of practice is that few injuries will be acquired.

Generally speaking, Tuesdays and Wednesdays are contact days, and Mondays and Thursdays are non-contact workouts. The schedule should vary as needed. We have found that it is advantageous to emphasize live work early in the season and to decrease the amount later.

It is advisable to conduct as much live work early in each practice as possible. There are studies that indicate that when players are tired, there is an increased chance for injury. Therefore, we believe you should warm up well, do the necessary live work, and finish with non-contact preparation.

COACHES—BE OUT EARLY

One of the best ways to encourage extra effort, punctuality, and interest is the coaches' early arrival at practice. A good procedure that will cultivate initiative on the part of coaches is for the head coach to lead assistants onfield each day. There is no reason why the entire staff cannot take the field together five minutes before early practice or specialists come out.

Asking the kids to get out early and work extra, while staff is still inside, is operating under a double standard. A sound football program is based on standards, principles, and philosophy conducive to fairness for all. The coaches' slogan "Don't expect of your players any more than you are willing to give yourself," exemplifies well why coaches should be on-field when footballers are. If you want the squad to respect and admire you, and maintain loyalty, give them something to look up to.

Coaches' procedure for early practice

There are three phases to early practice:

1) Discuss aspects of early practice with other coaches before pre-practice.
2) Jog onfield together. All coaches report to a predetermined area and in a group, but individually, loosen up.
3) Move to coaching stations and wait for footballers.

Each coach ought to have with him on the field a whistle, stopwatch, practice schedule, pencil, sunglasses, wristwatch, paper, and clipboard.

PREVENT INJURIES WITH COMMANDOS

Because of the wide-openness of a passing attack, men cutting and operating in the open field, passing and blocking executed from semi-stationary positions, injuries to leg joints are common. In any season, either ankles or knees will hamper a team at one time or another. To combat this nuisance, a few years ago our staff studied the problem and decided appropriate training and conditioning could help curb the number of these injuries. Our conclusion was based on the idea of strengthening muscle tissue around these joints.

The method chosen to accomplish this objective was two-fold. We would overload the muscles with continuous, rigorous work. Running in sand or uphill seemed to work best. A second approach is to have players run on the side of a hill. This activity places great strain on the muscles that support the joints. It will stretch the fiber and tone the muscles.

We designed a commando course that the squad is required to run before and after every practice. This course forces the footballers to run through one hundred yards of sand on the side of a hill eighty yards in length. Since this form of training was introduced in our practices, we have almost eliminated ankle and knee injuries.

ISOMETRICS IN PRACTICE

The purpose of isometric exercises is to develop a maximum amount of strength and stamina within a minimum amount of time. In our program, as suggested earlier, isometrics are used during the season as a substitute for weight training. We promote the theory that isometrics will not increase dimensions of muscle fiber to any degree, but will serve to help maintain the enlarged fiber already developed through weight training.

This type of exercise is done in a series of *bouts* which last for six seconds apiece. In every bout or specific activity there must be a maximum effort, or the exercise is valueless. Also isometric exercises are done at the end of each of our practices. The entire daily program takes but six or seven minutes. Using this concept of force against force or muscles versus muscles, we religiously participate in our Dirty Dozen Isometric Program, shown in Figure 16-4.

An aspect of isometrics worth mentioning is that they require no equipment. All force can be applied by another athlete. Add this factor to the limited time it takes to carry on a program, and isometrics become an even more effective training device.

LEARNING THROUGH PART AND WHOLE THEORY

With discussion of stressing various parts of the passing game, the question still remains as to how these phases relate

R = RESISTANCE   V = POINT OF RESISTANCE
→ = DIRECTION OF FORCE OR PRESSURE

**BICEPS
PRESS
6 SEC.**

**TRICEPS
PRESS
6 SEC.**

**PECTORALIS
PRESS
6 SEC.**

**FRONT FLEXOR
PRESS
6 SEC.**

**HYPEREXTENSION
PRESS
6 SEC.**

**HAMSTRING
PRESS
12 SEC.**

**QUADRICEPS
PRESS
12 SEC.**

**GASTROC
PRESS
6 SEC.**

**NECK
PRESS
24 SEC.**

FIGURE 16–4   FOOTBALL ISOMETRIC EXERCISES

to your practice schedule. Most authorities will agree that every practice needs teaching directed at the individual, small groups, and team. Development and learning is based upon this theory. Because this hypothesis is sound and widely accepted, we create our practice schedules around this concept. Each regular practice session emphasizes the Part and Whole Theory of Learning by providing drills that meet these objectives.

In practice there needs to be work that places the player in a coach-player (one-to-one) relationship. This learning situation should be followed by a coach-small group teaching situation. Lastly, the total or whole process of learning should be used. Our time blocks of teaching are at least fifteen minutes of individual work, forty minutes of group activity, and twenty minutes of team development.

A LAST REMINDER

Someone once said, "Watch a team practice, and you can predict the outcome of the next game." Though validity of this statement is unproven, there is reason to support it. Psychological and physiological tempo during practice does tend to indicate the readiness of a squad. Highly spirited practices reflect determination, desire, and morale. To win, these attributes must be present. Coaches cultivate and appeal to these qualities to make practices worthwhile and meaningful. Remember, a team's success depends upon its preparation; so build your passing game in practice.

17

Drills That Make
the Difference

Teaching football is reliance upon repeated exercises called drills. Drills lead to execution and perfection. The importance of utilizing drills in practice is without question a must in football today. Drills can serve a number of objectives. They can act as fundamental methods of teaching a skill. A drill might serve to develop reaction. Other drills tend to condition or toughen. Still other drills may be used solely for change-of-pace or fun purposes.

INTRODUCTION

Within the aforementioned categories of drills, specific phases of the passing game can be grouped. This chapter on drills attempts to provide not only a variety of useful drills, but a sound approach to their usage.

We feel that there are definite points that need stressing when installing drills. Footballers will get far more out of drill work if they know the how, what, and why of each. Therefore, when introducing a drill we like to be sure that those who will be using it know its purpose, how it functions, what is the starting command, and its name.

There are other important factors related to the administration of drills. Where the coach stands in a given drill is vital for proper execution and observation. Rotation of players in drills is most important for correct function. These things must be known about each drill if their utilization is to play any role in a team's practice sessions.

Of all aspects of adopting drills, the most important consideration is that each be as game-like as possible. The idea of having drill for the sake of drill is ridiculous. Each drill used should be accurately realistic. This is imperative for the carry-over value a drill instills.

SELECTED AREA FOR DRILL

Drills can be more efficiently conducted if players and coaches know the designated places for their execution. We divide the practice field into five drill stations—for offensive backs, interior linemen, receivers, passers, and team development. As described in Chapter 16, "How to Build Your Passing Game in Practice," these areas of the field are labeled with the letters of the alphabet.

DEMONSTRATE BEFORE EXECUTION

A good habit any coach should develop when introducing a drill is to demonstrate procedure. It is much easier for players to grasp a drill if they have seen it executed. Demonstration must stress objectives and technique and should include: (1) Oral explanation of drill; (2) Walking through steps; and (3) Full-scale active demonstration. As these are concluded, emphasis on technique can be highlighted. This is done by summarizing drill procedure. An example is stay low, head up, body under control, feet shoulder width, eyes open, neck bulled, and so forth.

Instruction, preceded by exhibition regarding second-effort aspects of the exercise, should follow initial teaching of the drill.

This might mean simply sprinting back to the end of a line. More often, however, it means accomplishing a second task, since most good drills attempt to develop second effort.

It is suggested that coaches who cannot effectively demonstrate a drill not try to do so. Instead, call upon a capable player, captain, or fellow coach. It is also recommended that bags, dummies, sleds, and other teaching apparatus, rather than players, be used when demonstrating.

INSIST ON DISCIPLINE IN DRILLS

One of the fastest ways to chaos in a drill is to permit fooling around. We recommend keeping players in lines whenever possible. In addition, we discipline those who talk to others during a drill. Our staff insists upon hustle and all-out performance every minute. Above all, we never permit a player to execute a drill incorrectly, no matter how many times it takes him to do it right.

DEVELOP MORALE AND ENTHUSIASM

There are many approaches to developing spirit in drills. Regardless, a coach must first convince players that drills will help improve their play. After footballers accept this, they must see results. They want to see their progress on a chart, know they are executing a skill faster or blocking better. Besides the youngster himself knowing of improvement, it is wise to keep other players posted. We have found that, by constantly praising a player for his improvement, he will continue to do better. When this pride in accomplishment is motivated in a few players, the entire squad will be affected and uplifted.

BE ORGANIZED—TEN CONSIDERATIONS FOR DRILLING

If the following points are considered, the value of the drill method of teaching will be heightened, interest and enthusiasm produced, and morale cultivated. Practice sessions will become meaningful and significant.

No. 1: Drills function better if they are kept short and progressive. Most drills can fulfill their purpose in a five-minute period. Activities lasting longer should be repeated less frequently to discourage boredom.

No. 2: Equipment for drill should be available at coaching station prior to player arrival. Items like dummies, air bags, sled, tires, ropes, footballs, ought to be convenient for immediate use.

No. 3: All players run to and from drill area. Stragglers must be disciplined. Coach responsible for drill should lead group to station.

No. 4: Before introducing drill, demonstrate procedure or technique.

No. 5: Injured players should be checked before allowing participation in drill. There are some drills that certain casualties can compete in.

No. 6: Be sure goals are being met and drill is realistic.

No. 7: At some time during each drill have something positive to say about each player.

No. 8: Use starting count to begin drills and whistle to end them.

No. 9: Never allow too many footballers to be working in drill at same time. Remember your eyes can only see so much.

No. 10: Coach should position himself in most advantageous position possible to witness activity.

TYPES OF DRILLS

For convenience, drills are grouped into three classifications: passing, receiving, and pass protection. Symbols are used for description and clarification purposes. The following is a list of symbols, and their meanings, shown in the diagrams of activities later in this chapter:

R	Receiver	B	Blocker
P	Passer	V	Defensivemen
C	Coach	A	Air bag
D	Dummies	T	Tackler

Any drill that involves pass patterns can also be used for pass defense. As receivers run their routes, defenders can perfect coverage techniques. Adding defensive personnel also tends to make a drill more realistic, since under game conditions plays will be executed against other players.

FIGURE 17–1   STEP UP (PASSERS)

1) Quarterback takes exchange, drops back, sets up, and steps up.
2) Defensive ends rush to set-up position of quarterback.
3) Ends tag back of quarterback as they run by passer.

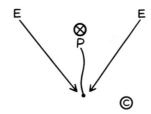

FIGURE 17–2   PICK IT UP AND THROW (PASSERS)

1) Passer drops back without ball, picks up ball from ground, and continues drop-back technique.
2) Quarterback sets up and throws to receiver.

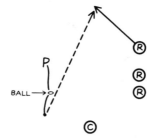

FIGURE 17–3   PASSING UNDER PRESSURE (PASSERS)

1) Passer takes exchange and sets up to throw.
2) Defensive players, with air bags, delay two to four counts (depending on depth of pattern) and rush passer.
3) Defensive man tags quarterback with air bag, but does not knock him down.

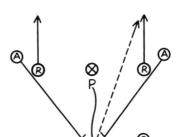

FIGURE 17-4   DUMP THE BALL (PASSERS)

1) Passer reads two defensive men and receiver.
2) Receiver runs streak or out pattern.
3) If receiver is covered, passer over-leads receiver.
4) Emphasis of drill—to prevent interceptions and stop clock.
5) Ball is thrown only if receiver is open.

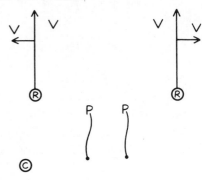

FIGURE 17-5   STANDING CIRCLE (PASSERS)

1) Passers rotate around a standing man and throw to him.
2) Stationary man tosses ball back.
3) Good warm-up drill.
4) Cuts down on amount of running passers must do.

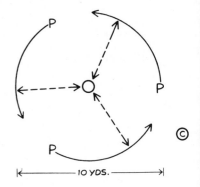

FIGURE 17-6   DIRECTION (PASSERS)

1) Passer drops back and sets.
2) As Passer sets, coach calls right or left.
3) Passer steps and throws to receiver in direction of call.
4) Coach watches for proper throwing technique and body position.

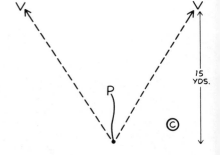

FIGURE 17–7   FEEL THE BALL (PASSERS)

1) Quarterbacks toss and catch ball one-handed.
2) Passers concentrate on good hand position on ball.

FIGURE 17–8   LOOK AT ME (PASSERS)

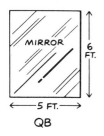

1) Quarterbacks line up, in stance, facing mirror.
2) Execution of ball, position, grip, feet should be studied.
3) Sprint-out and drop-back procedure can be practiced.

FIGURE 17–9   PLAY CATCH (PASSERS)

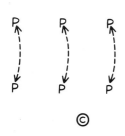

1) Passers throw to each other.
2) Good warm-up drill.

FIGURE 17–10   ONE KNEE DOWN (PASSERS)

1) Passer puts knee on ground and throws to other quarterback.
2) Right-handed passer, right knee down— left-handed passer, left knee.
3) Stress passing form and technique.
4) Good warm-up drill.

FIGURE 17–11   JUDGMENT (PASSERS)

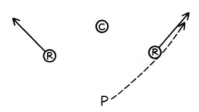

1) Passer looks in one direction, then another, and throws in that direction.
2) Pass should be less than twenty yards.

FIGURE 17–12   THROWING ON TIME (PASSERS)

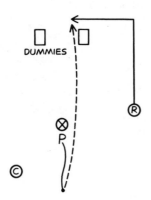

1) Passer times receiver's pattern.
2) Throws ball between dummies with proper lead.

FIGURE 17–13   CATCH ONE (RECEIVERS AND PASSERS)

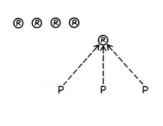

1) Three passers throw balls at receiver at once.
2) Receiver tries to catch one.

FIGURE 17–14   FORM DRILL (RECEIVERS AND PASSERS)

1) Receivers run any pass pattern desired.
2) Passer works on throwing.
3) Without receivers, passer may practice
on form by throwing into net.

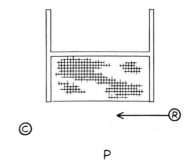

FIGURE 17–15   THUMBS-IN DRILL (RECEIVERS AND PASSERS)

1) Passer throws ball at receiver and over
his head.
2) Receiver runs toward passer and catches
ball with thumbs "in."

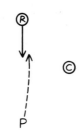

FIGURE 17–16   TIP DRILL (RECEIVERS)

1) Ball is thrown high over head of receiver, who hits it up in air.
2) Two other receivers go for ball.

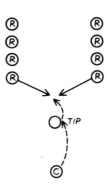

FIGURE 17–17   HOLD ON (PASSERS)

1) One passer holds ball in one hand for
about five seconds.
2) Then, ball is thrown to another passer.
3) Second passer repeats holding ball five
seconds, then returns throw.

FIGURE 17–18   LOOSEN UP (PASSERS)

1) Passers space themselves ten yards apart and behind each other, all facing in same direction.
2) On command of last passer, they run straight ahead. Last passer throws ball to man to the side and in front of him, who throws to next man, etc.
3) When ball reaches front man, all turn and run drill in opposite direction.

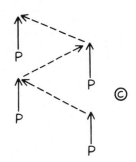

FIGURE 17–19   SPRINT-OUT PASSING (PASSERS)

1) Passer runs option pass—throws if defensive man pressures, runs if receiver covered.
2) Next passer, receiver, and defensive halfback repeat drill.

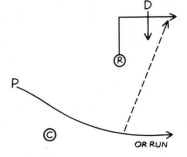

FIGURE 17–20   TIRE DRILL (PASSERS)

1) Passer uses either drop-back technique or set position.
2) Passer throws through swinging tire.

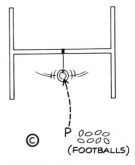

FIGURE 17–21   SETTING UP/BY THE COUNT (QUARTERBACKS)

1) Quarterback takes exchange and sets up in either two- or four-count set.
2) Drop-back form and body position are checked.

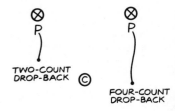

FIGURE 17–22 BRING THE BALL OVER (QUARTERBACKS)

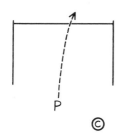

1) A bar is placed at shoulder height.
2) Standing near bar, quarterback passes over it.
3) Drill helps quarterback throwing ball over his head.

FIGURE 17–23 DROP-BACK DRILL NO. 1 (QUARTERBACKS)

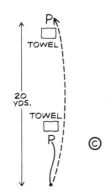

1) Quarterback sets in exchange position facing off another quarterback.
2) Proper count and drop-back procedure are stressed.
3) Passer throws to another quarterback.
4) Receiver checks passer's form.

FIGURE 17–24 DROP-BACK DRILL NO. 2 (QUARTERBACKS)

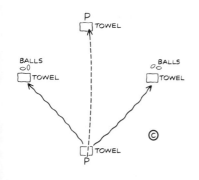

1) Same as No. 1, but receiver runs to one of towels on release count.
2) Quarterback sets up and throws.

FIGURE 17-25   SCREEN DRILL (QUARTERBACKS)

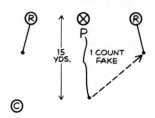

1) Either of two receivers may be set in backfield or flanked.
2) Quarterback may practice timing, fakes, and footwork.

FIGURE 17-26   READ PRESSURE (QUARTERBACKS)

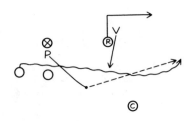

1) Passer sprints out with ball chest high, ready to throw.
2) If pressure, passer throws to back in motion.
3) If no pressure, throws to end or runs.

FIGURE 17-27   HANDS, EYES, AND TOUCH DRILL (QUARTERBACKS)

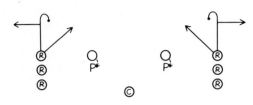

1) Quarterback receives ball tossed quickly to him.
2) Then, he throws to receiver.

FIGURE 17-28   EXCHANGE DRILL (QUARTERBACKS)

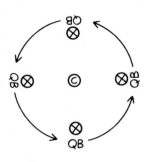

1) On command, all quarterbacks start count, stressing proper timing and count method.
2) Each quarterback takes exchange and sprints to next center.

FIGURE 17–29 LINE DRILL (QUARTERBACKS)

1) Two quarterbacks run the line.
2) They throw as they run.

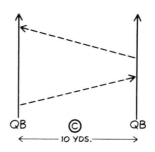

FIGURE 17–30 CIRCLE DRILL (QUARTERBACKS)

1) Two passers run in a circle.
2) They throw to each other.

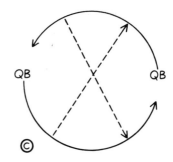

FIGURE 17–31 RUNNING THE LINE (RECEIVERS)

1) At full speed, receivers run various routes chalked on grass.
2) Practice cuts and timing.

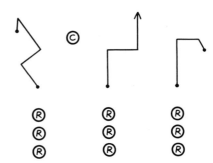

FIGURE 17–32   OBSTACLES (RECEIVERS)

1) Receiver starts from stance, scrambles through dummies.
2) Completes a forward roll, huddles a dummy lying on ground.
3) After huddling dummy, two to four steps are taken and a cut into pattern is taken.
4) Ball thrown by passer in accordance with timing of play.

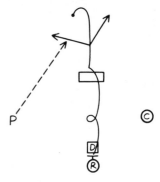

FIGURE 17–33   CATCH THE HARD ONE (RECEIVERS)

1) Passer calls right or left and receiver runs accordingly.
2) Passer throws ball low, high, or behind, or far ahead.
3) Receiver's technique is observed and coached.

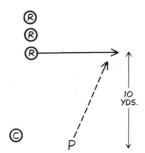

FIGURE 17–34   GET HIT (RECEIVERS)

1) Receivers run pattern toward defender.
2) Defender with air bag hits receiver just after cut and as he catches ball.

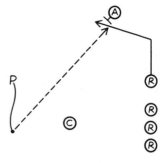

FIGURE 17–35   BE READY (RECEIVERS)

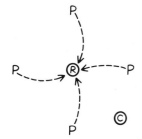

1) Receiver lies on back.
2) On whistle, he jumps to feet and looks for ball.
3) Ball is thrown by one of four passers facing him.
4) Coach designates who will pass.

FIGURE 17–36   RELEASE (RECEIVERS)

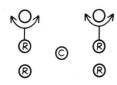

1) Receivers set in stance.
2) Coach calls cadence and receivers fire on count.
3) Receivers taught how to get by defender and into pattern.
4) Defensive men do all in their power to prevent release of offensive men.

FIGURE 17–37   POSITION ON DEFENDERS (RECEIVERS)

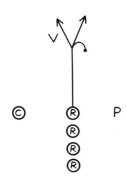

1) Receiver runs downfield and breaks in any direction he chooses.
2) His main objective is to cut in a direction that allows best possible position on defenders.

FIGURE 17–38   BRING IT DOWN (RECEIVERS)

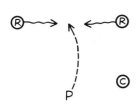

1) Ball is thrown high between two receivers.
2) Both receivers go high for the ball.

FIGURE 17–39   FIRST MOVE TECHNIQUE (RECEIVERS)

1) Man carrying dummy runs at receiver while receiver sprints toward dummy.
2) Before reaching dummy, receiver makes a move and breaks into a pattern.

FIGURE 17–40   BODY CONTROL (RECEIVERS)

1) Receiver runs down line, weaving from side to side.
2) He carries ball and changes it from arm to arm.

FIGURE 17–41   GET FREE (RECEIVERS)

1) Starting from stance, receiver releases by defender any way possible.
2) Various release techniques can be practiced.
3) Ball can be thrown to receiver as soon as he gets by defensive man.

FIGURE 17–42   IT'S MINE (RECEIVERS)

1) Passer throws ball high between two receivers.
2) Both receivers go for ball.
3) Position and aggressiveness are emphasized.

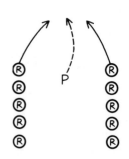

FIGURE 17–43   LOOK UP (RECEIVERS)

1) Receiver runs at heavy bag and jumps over.
2) As soon as receiver's feet hit ground, passer delivers ball.

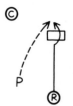

FIGURE 17-44   DIVE (RECEIVERS)

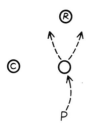

1) Passer throws ball soft and high to a player, who hits ball in air in one direction or another.
2) Receiver, standing directly behind, reacts to ball.
3) Receiver may be standing or running in this drill, in which catching the ball is all important. Diving catches are common.

FIGURE 17-45   HANDS UP (RECEIVERS)

1) Receiver releases downfield.
2) One of passers on either side can throw ball immediately.
3) Receiver must react and catch ball from whichever side it's thrown.

FIGURE 17-46   BIG EFFORT (RECEIVERS)

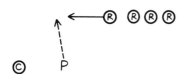

1) Receiver runs straight line and is thrown ball beyond his reach.
2) Receiver is expected to extend himself and dive for ball.
3) Passer should throw soft pass.

FIGURE 17-47   OVER THE SHOULDER (RECEIVERS)

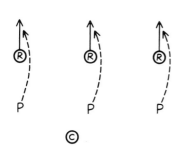

1) From stance, receiver sprints away from passer.
2) Passer throws ball high and with lead.
3) Receiver runs under ball and catches it over his shoulder.

FIGURE 17-48   CUT-OFF (RECEIVERS)

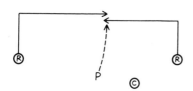

1) Passer throws ball down middle of drill.
2) One receiver runs in front of another and catches ball, moving in opposite direction.

FIGURE 17–49   SCRAMBLE RELEASE (RECEIVERS)

1) From stance, receiver scrambles through two heavy dummies, held by players on an angle.
2) Holders of dummies should offer resistance.

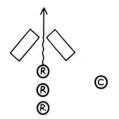

FIGURE 17–50   CATCH/TAKE ON DEFENDER (RECEIVERS)

1) Catch ball and either take on tackler or break away from him.
2) Tackler should be instructed to form tackle.

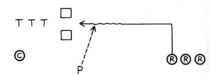

FIGURE 17–51   YOU AND ME (LINEMEN)

1) Offensive men pass block as long and hard as possible.
2) Defensive men must stay between bags and rush to dummies.
3) Can use watch in this drill.

FIGURE 17–52   RECOVER (LINEMEN)

1) Offensive man starts on knees, facing defensive man.
2) On starting count, defensive man delays one to two counts and rushes.
3) Offensive lineman scrambles to football position and takes on pass rusher.

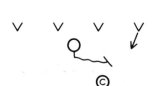

FIGURE 17–53   TAKE 'EM ALL (LINEMEN)

1) Blocker takes on one man chosen by coach.
2) As soon as block has been made, coach calls for another man to rush.
3) Rushers are numbered—coach merely calls out number.

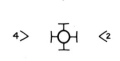

FIGURE 17–54   GET BIG (LINEMEN)

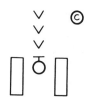

1) Blocker takes on both rushers and prevents them from penetrating.
2) Pass block technique is used as long as possible, then cross-body or another type of block may be used.

FIGURE 17–55   COUNT-OFF BLOCKING (LINEMEN)

1) Linemen pass block by counting off defensive men from center to outside.
2) Form, technique, and position should be stressed.

FIGURE 17–56   SPRINT-OUT BLOCKING (GUARDS)

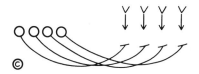

1) Guards pull and get proper depth.
2) They turn upfield and take on defenders.
3) Defenders can use air bags if desired.

FIGURE 17–57   AREA BLOCKING (LINEMEN)

1) On starting count, blockers block man on, forcing defenders inside, if possible.
2) Blockers must not allow linebackers to rush inside gaps.
3) Blockers may block man on and a linebacker, if linebacker rush is to inside gap. If linebacker rush is to outside gap, blockers do not react out.

FIGURE 17–58   READ AND BLOCK (LINEMEN)

1) On starting count, blocker reacts as if to pass block.
2) Reads proper man and blocks him.
3) Both defenders will feint a rush, but only one is told to rush by the coach.

FIGURE 17–59   READING THE RUSH (LINEMEN)

1) Five interior linemen read defense and pass block according to offensive call.
2) If offensive call is on area call, each lineman picks up man or men in area. If number call, guards block first man to their side of center; tackles block second man, while center always blocks area.
3) Coach calls blocking assignments.

FIGURE 17–60   PICKING UP THE LOOSE MAN (LINEMEN)

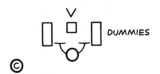

DUMMIES

1) Defensive man rips into heavy bag and continues rush to either side, but inside dummies.
2) Offensive man reads situation, picks up man, and pass blocks him.

FIGURE 17–61   ME VERSUS YOU (LINEMEN)

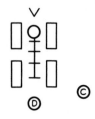

1) Blocker pass blocks as long and hard as possible.
2) Position and technique are stressed. Stopwatch may be used.

FIGURE 17–62   MEND THE CUP (LINEMEN AND BACKS)

1) Blocker reacts to man selected by coach to rush.
2) Reading, reacting, and position of blocker are emphasized.

USE OF CHARTS IN EVALUATING DRILLS

Coaches often are critical of players' mistakes made during a game. In many instances these criticisms are justifiable. However, how often do coaches analyze and evaluate the amount of teaching time spent on the skill that might have prevented the mistake? A chart can act as a standing record of time spent on a given drill. There is little doubt that the more time spent, the more perfect a skill will become.

Charting drills can be broken down into three categories: Team Drills; Line Play; and Backfield Play. A recommended chart size is 18x30 inches. This size provides a desirable recording surface. It is large enough to be eye-catching, yet small enough to be placed on almost any wall. The chart should list drills in a column to the left and provide a place to record time spent on a drill to the right. Days of the week should be placed across the top. The use of colored pencils and marking pens adds to its effectiveness.

Another feature necessary in maintaining an effective chart is proper organization of drills. This should include correct grouping, as indicated above. Each drill should have a name and be classified according to its value.

If charts are to be effective, they should be checked regularly. Weekly evaluation is recommended to help in the planning of the following week's practice schedule. A seasonal evaluation aids in determining time spent on specific drills during the year. It also serves as a means to check the value *derived* from time spent on these drills throughout the past season.

THERE IS NO SUBSTITUTE FOR DRILL

Drills act as an "instrument" or means of teaching. They provide the stage upon which various phases of football are taught. The type, amount, and method of implementation of drills are in direct relation to the productivity of your team. Through drills, a sound fundamental knowledge and understanding of techniques necessary for execution of skills can be instilled.

PERFECTION IS THE END RESULT OF DRILLS

18

How to Succeed
As a Coach

Those who are believers in an all-out passing offense are of a different breed. We are considered radical in theory and non-conformist in nature. No doubt there are a few who call us mavericks, and perhaps they fear the beginning of the end for the hard-nosed grind-it-out or precision style of offensive play.

Teaching the forward pass concept of football requires new ideas, unique approaches, and above all, imagination. Coaches must be individualistic, original, forceful, flexible, and enthusiastic. We purposely have left the word "organizational" for last, since the primary role of the head coach is to organize and pull together the aforementioned attributes. The effectiveness of any offense depends upon utilization of these qualities, but they are especially important when instituting a passing philosophy.

THE FUNCTION OF A HEAD COACH

The qualifications of a top-notch head football coach are comparable to those of an officer in the service, an administrator in an educational program, and a politician, all in one.

He must be tactful, resourceful, personable, and as already mentioned above, he must possess the rare gift of being able to organize. Does it sound like few of us can qualify? How wrong! The coaching profession probably has more skilled and talented people than any other group. How many men dedicate as much time as coaches do? There is no question that directing a football program places unbelievable demands on a man. Because football is so complex, functionability depends on organization. Every minute detail of a program has to be considered. No objective can be reached if there is not, first, a course of action from which to progress. Planning involves coordinating each aspect of football in harmonious order.

An orderly, well-planned program allows for maximum effectiveness, while operating in the shortest possible time. As chief organizer, the head coach must devote a phenomenal amount of time to the endeavor. Arranging a football program takes three shapes—to be considered are *coaches, players,* and *others associated with the program.* All three of these have been discussed before, but it should be established here' that a head man's job is to organize these people. His future depends upon it.

A complete job description of a head football coach involves a wide scope of technical information, as well as broad knowledge of football. Detection of needs, and ability to analyze and evaluate are among the main tasks of a skipper. More specifically, the role of a head coach is:

1) Along with assistants, interpret policies of the athletic program and implement them in the best manner possible.

2) Cooperate with the school administration, other coaches, and the chairman of the athletic department on matters concerning athletics.

3) Have a knowledgeable account of league, section, and state rules regarding football.

4) Be responsible for budgeting, selecting, and maintaining of all football equipment.

5) Supervise duties of assistant coaches.

6) Create realistic standards and objectives from which a healthy football program can mature. In conjunction with the staff, see that the previously mentioned rules are adhered to.

7) With assistants, establish a plan of action to include daily, weekly, and seasonal practice schedules that effectively implement the entire system of football.

8) Determine appropriate drills and procedures that best teach the various phases of the program.

9) Select and supervise the work of student assistants and managers.

10) Assume responsibility for first aid applied on the practice field, report injuries to a doctor, and follow-up work done on each injury.

11) Be directly responsible for player conduct in games, on the practice field, in the locker room, during team meetings, and while traveling to and from games.

12) Be indirectly responsible for the conduct and attitude of each player regardless of his whereabouts.

13) Choose appropriate awards for players and managers and make recommendations for special recognition.

14) Determine that all football players are insured properly.

15) Meet frequently with parents and interested citizens to promote the football program.

16) Maintain sound relationships with press and radio.

17) Inspect regularly all equipment for safety and cleanliness.

18) Select squad members and assign positions for each.

19) Conduct meetings involving the staff and players.

20) Attend league coaching meetings, clinics, and conferences that have to do with football.

21) Keep up on current football literature.

22) Coordinate efforts of the junior varsity program and other football programs that are part of the school system.

23) Exemplify an image that will reflect well upon the program.

ABOVE ALL, THE HEAD COACH MUST BE ABLE TO SELL HIMSELF IF HE IS TO SELL THE FOOTBALL PROGRAM.

A MESSAGE TO ASSISTANTS

No head coach is any better than those with whom he works—his assistants. Assistants can set the tone, and project positiveness or despair in a football program. The actions of staff members directly affect the kids, and indirectly the school and community.

A situation, no matter how bad, can be improved by a hard-working, dedicated, and loyal staff. When coaches believe in themselves and their abilities, no barriers are too big, no problems unsolvable. A closely knit group of coaches can elevate a program far beyond its potential, with leadership and good public relations.

Apathy and discontent are more trying enemies than any opponent a team meets, for these are the elements that breed failure. There is no room for this "disease" in any program. It is the responsibility of those who direct a program, *the coaches*, to set the example, establish the climate, and produce the environment from which a healthy football program can grow. Since the atmosphere of a program stems from its principles and standards, there must first be a common agreement on philosophy. All coaches must trust one another—being loyal to what they represent through their actions and deeds.

Praise the head coach

It should be remembered that your personal success depends upon the success of the head man. What you do for him, you do for yourself. His future is your future. Building his image is like putting money in the bank. Good assistants are constantly praising the efforts of the head coach and those affiliated with the program. An assistant is a good-will ambassador.

Carry your weight

There is no room in any program for dead wood. Part of the job of an assistant is to project a favorable image. The clothing worn, as well as personal mannerisms, are indicative to all with whom you come in contact. Sloppy habits reflect on the football program. It's hard to impress anyone if you yourself are not impressive. It's surprising what the proper image can do for your program. *You play as you look!*

REWARD FOR SERVICE

To insure that coaching morale will stay at a peak, assistant coaches need to be constantly rewarded for their service. This reward can take a number of forms; credit and praise at rallies, recognition in local press, radio, and kind words about coaches to a squad, all help accomplish this feat.

At the conclusion of each season, a nominal gift to each assistant helps prove your gratitude for their efforts. But perhaps the most popular and successful method to acquire and stimulate good relations is to present a small token of appreciation to the wives of each staff member. When wives are behind the program, all is well. Christmas, the end of the season, at a banquet or just an informal call can serve as the occasion for making this gesture.

CONDUCTING STAFF MEETINGS

All organization begins in your coaching meetings. Here is where ideas are exchanged, program evaluated, and decisions made. It is also where the coaches can gain fellowship and become closely linked. These meetings can serve to cement relationships and loyalties far beyond those shared by ordinary friends.

We contend that the most appropriate meeting night is Monday. Sunday meetings tend to interfere with family plans and are complicated by last week's game film, which probably is not yet completely rated and evaluated. In addition, scouting information on next week's opponent possibly is not yet broken down into seasonal tendencies. The weekend al-

lows time to accomplish these objectives. Monday is about as
early as needed to begin formulating the next game plan.

The most desirable location for meeting is the home of the
head coach (providing there are proper facilities). By holding
the meetings there, refreshments are at hand and the comfort of a home has an advantage over an office or classroom.
Getting together in the home of the head man creates a warm
atmosphere conducive to productivity and comradeship.

Coaching meetings should be divided into two areas of concentration. Experience has taught us that about one-third of
the meeting time is enough to evaluate last week's game (assuming individual player ratings have been done). The remaining two-thirds of the time may be spent concentrating on
the coming game. A three-hour meeting normally is sufficent
to complete the business at hand.

A supply of pencils, paper, blackboard, and chalk make up
basic supplies needed at every meeting. Having a projector
analyzer on hand is a good practice since there is occasionally
need to refer to a play or situation on film. Each coach is asked
to keep a notebook, in which notes from each meeting are kept,
along with game plans and scouting information on each team.

ORGANIZATION OF MEETINGS

If the head coach does all the suggesting and makes all the
decisions, there is no need for getting together. Meetings must
feature involvement. Because of this, each coach on the staff
should have some specific responsibilities. In each meeting,
each coach dominates his area of responsibility. The scouting
report presentation on a certain team might be the job of
one coach, while fellow coaches have other teams to concentrate on. The task of breaking down film is still another's responsibility. Presenting a film analysis and rating players should
be done by the coach directly assigned to that phase; this means
the backfield coach ranking backs and the line coach rating
linemen. Grades of players are presented by these coaches.

By using the whole staff, individual coaches develop a sense of belonging. They take pride in their work. This utilization of staff not only promotes good morale, but allows for completeness in each aspect of organization. Specific jobs are done better when one man is responsible for them.

SPECIAL MEETINGS

During the season, we hold daily meetings with the squad during lunch period. Players are asked to bring their lunches to these meetings. The meetings encompass:

Monday	Film of last week's game.
Tuesday	Scouting report on opponent (quarterback get game plan).
Wednesday	Game plan—defense stressed.
Thursday	Review scouting reports.
Friday	Last-minute instructions; pre-game plan; psychology to be used; traveling instruction if needed.

It is also necessary to have other regular meetings to plan for daily practices. These get-togethers can be held during common prep periods. We have found that these meetings foster a great deal of socialization which is desirable, but often another meeting must be held prior to practice.

Certain aspects of coaching responsibilities will occasionally require a conference between an assistant coach and the skipper. It is a sound approach to get together to discuss these specific facets of football. This will help relations and encourage articulation of teaching.

LEARNING NEVER STOPS

Attending clinics and keeping up on current football literature is not enough. A well-informed coach should visit as many college spring football practices as possible. Observing the tactics and methods of a college staff can be most profitable. Some schools will allow you to sit in on planning sessions or other meetings. Each member of our staff tries to attend at least one day of a college team's spring practice. The ideas and information obtained there are shared with the rest of our staff on returning.

Another very useful and rewarding experience is to spend a day with a good coach whom you admire and respect. Since we are advocates of the aerial game, we have pursued those who preach and teach the same general philosophy. Many of our innovations and ideas have come from these men.

OFF-SEASON MEETINGS

Football is no longer a sport that simply requires attendance during the season. It takes a year-round effort to do an effective job. Off-season meetings are designed to evaluate last year's campaign and plan for the coming season. This is done from the week after football ends until the task is completed. The evaluation portion of meetings is primarily geared to grading each player and ranking his potential in relation to the coming season. Films provide a basis for evaluation. Hopefully, this job is finished by the first of the year.

Beginning in January, it is advisable to renew weekly meetings with the prime function being to hash over offensive and defensive concepts. Changes in philosophy and organization are made now. Practice and scouting assignment schedules and off-season training should be discussed and absorbed by the staff.

There is a lot of merit in setting aside one meeting per month as a time to build morale. Wives can be asked to attend. The affair should not be one of business, but rather a social event. A barbeque, picnic, dinner, or simple party can provide the desired friendly atmosphere.

BUILDING FOR TOMORROW

A coach's job must be not only to mold today's team, but to shape tomorrow's. It is not enough for a football program to advocate an aerial game; it must instill this philosophy in the entire community and, more important, in the youth. To promote the passing game community wide is a responsibility of the coaching staff. Be it a local Pop Warner team, the junior high football squad, or just an interested group, the passing game philosophy has to be implanted. Working closely with these groups will result in a better program in the seasons to come.

A good policy each year is to provide these other community teams with a copy of your offense. Inviting the coaches to meetings can also be helpful in accomplishing your promotional objectives. Maintaining the belief in and support of throwing the ball is a never-ending job about which coaches must be continually concerned.

BE ACTIVE IN COMMUNITY AFFAIRS

No football program is strong enough to stand alone. The more the community support, the stronger the program. Community backing and enthusiasm is built in part by team performance, but most likely by personal appeal. People who know the coach, and like him, will support him. It is therefore advisable to be active in community affairs. *Go where the people go. Do what they do. Join clubs that serve the people. Participate in worthwhile charity drives. Take in community socials. Attend church regularly.*

The relationships that can be formed through these activities will reward the coach many times over. Remember, you must be part of something before you are considered involved and accepted. Our experience has shown that if you will meet people half way, they will come the other half.

STIMULATE PRIDE

What is pride? It is the dedication and loyalty one has toward something. It is personal concern about what a person believes in. Pride is not something you are born with. Rather it is a quality that has to be nurtured. To a football team, pride is essential. From season to season, game to game, this intangible feeling elevates a team's morale or causes chaos. Since obviously a club must have pride to win, and is something that is developed, a program must have an established approach to its creation.

The first step is to make football the most recognized and supported phase of the educational program. The game must be accepted and backed by community and school. If these two groups support football, those who play will have pride in knowing they represent people who care about them. Developing pride begins with promotion of interest in the community and school. Methods to influence and create enthusiasm are varied in nature and should depend on the circumstances within a given community.

These are some successful techniques used to secure support through active campaign or promotion:

Get your faculty behind the program

Faculty backing is most important. These people are close to the kids and the program. Their acceptance or rejection establishes the tone or climate of football development. Fellow teachers help coaches earn their keep. How the teachers speak of football, the players, and coaches is interpreted by the whole student body and diffused into the community. Without faculty support, a team is in trouble. Coaches and players alike must cultivate good relationships with teachers if good feeling is to prevail elsewhere.

Make games entertaining

Nature of performance has a definite bearing on spectator support. We are not suggesting that you must win to have a large, enthusiastic following. Winning helps, of course; but what really brings people to the contest is the style of play. It has been expressed in Chapter 1, but is worth emphasizing again—People love excitement. They want to see long passes, good runs, and many touchdowns. All these make the game colorful.

Identity

Everyone wants to be part of something that will give them prestige or status. Association with a football program can supply this desire. A technique effective for stimulating pride is providing identity for each member of squad with a blazer jacket. It is amazing how impressive a tie and coat can be to others. The image projected through this gentlemanly look is quite becoming. If coaches and faculty participate by wearing a blazer, it will add even more identity. Game day can be dress-up day!

Establish an active Boosters Club

Here is the group that can really help create pride. Our Boosters Club has provided us with trophies for Lineman and Back of the Week, purchased film for games, and worked generally for the promotion of football. We have had Boosters Club members speak at rallies, make award presentations at halftimes of our games, discuss our football program at service club meetings, and plan our football banquet. The value of this group is unmeasurable.

Where promotion counts

The greatest promoters a football program can have are its players. Footballers are influenced by their coaches. Sound principles and standards, instilled in players, reflect on the school and community. A positive impression made by the kids is a good form of promotion. As each group of young men leaves football by way of graduation, they take with them a part of their coach. Thus they, like those on the team, are football ambassadors.

Advertising through information

To keep boosters and parents of footballers informed about the football program, a steady flow of publicity and information must continually be circulated. A series of letters in the winter and spring, presenting ideas and philosophy of program, is most helpful. An example of letters can be found in an article by this author in the April, 1965 issue of *Athletic Journal*. In the summer a booklet outlining plans for coming season, practice, and game schedules, as well as highlights of activities to come, is received with great enthusiasm.

All the kids must play

It is difficult to be proud of something you are not part of. Most young men do not go out for football to sit on the bench and watch others play—anyone can buy a ticket and do that. Pride begins with involvement. All must share the reward of playing. How long and when players participate is up to the coach, but if they don't play, dissension is the common result.

BE A RECRUITER

The destiny of a college coach is dependent upon his ability to recruit football players. Most high school coaches are limited either by rules or regulations in procuring athletes. This being so, high school recruiting must take a different form. Instead of enticing footballers from other districts or areas, recruiting must be done among the kids already in your particular school.

We estimate that about one-third of the top ten percent of athletes on a high school level never participate in football. This guess may vary depending on the size of the school and type of football program, but there is no doubt that in all schools, many good potential players do not turn out for football.

RELATIONS WITH THE PRESS

It goes without saying that the football program's relationship with the press is extremely important. Good coverage in the local paper is by far the best method of promoting the game. When sound, positive publicity is offered, football is elevated.

There are numerous approaches to establishing good relations with the press. Any method, however, hinges on the head coach's association and personality. Manner, humor, and thoughtfulness are keys. We have found when we keep the press informed of developments, they reciprocate with good coverage. Our methods of providing information to the press are as follows: (a) Press Conference. The press conference may be called by the coach at a predetermined time to release some specifics about the program. Another form of press conference is one that occurs following a game or practice. It is wise to provide a warm atmosphere if possible, with cold soft drinks or coffee. (b) Press Day. It is more appropriate and productive to hold a Press Day at least once in the early season. This function allows newspapermen to visit with the team while accumulating data. On this day we have our kids wear game uniforms and put on a normal pre-game warm-up. The public is invited, which provides an audience, again helping to promote the program. Our Boosters Club serves refreshments. (c) Press Release. A most common method of keeping the press informed is by way of a Press Release Form. This simple form is extremely basic in nature (see Figure 18-1). Included on it are places for name of writer and newspaper, name of person releasing material, date of release, subject, and content of material.

A gesture that helps cement relations with the press is providing the local sports writer and his family with season passes. Still another practice is to invite the press to the football banquet at the end of the season. These little things may be the determining factors in establishing good relations with the press.

These techniques are all proven methods and will surely help promote good coverage. A word of caution may be interjected here regarding the manner of negotiating with sports writers. Like coaches, they have a job to do. If you help them do a good job, they in turn will help you.

FIGURE 18–1   PRESS MEMO

To _____

From _____   Date _____

Subject _____

Content

THE DIFFICULT ROLE

Playing the role of a coach is not easy. For you, there is no guarantee that what is best will prevail regardless. The success or failure of every football program depends upon those who direct it. Direct well, for the secret to being a good coach is winning games—IT'S IN YOUR HANDS!

Index